Something's Burning

A comedy

Eric Chappell

Samuel French — London
New York - Toronto - Hollywood

CHARACTERS

Nell Adams, early 40s
Gail, Nell's sister, late 20s
Helen, late 30s
George, Helen's husband, late 30s-early 40s
Jim, late 50s

The action of the play takes place in the drawing-room and terrace garden of Nell Adams' house

Time — the present

SYNOPSIS OF SCENES

ACT I

ACT II

SOMETHING'S BURNING

First presented in an earlier version at the Theatre Royal,
Windsor, on the 14th April 1992, with the following cast:

George Rush	Christopher Blake
Nell Adams	Joanna Van Gyseghem
Jim Grant	Geoffrey Davis

Directed by Mark Piper
Designed by Alexander McPherson
Lighting by Mark Doubleday

Also by Eric Chappell,
published by Samuel French Ltd

Haunted
Haywire
Heatstroke
It Can Damage Your Health
Natural Causes
Theft

ACT I
SCENE 1

The drawing-room and terrace garden of Nell Adams' house. Spring. Evening

The drawing-room is US. *A window in the* US *wall overlooks the drive. A door* UR *leads to the hall. A door* DC, *facing* R, *leads on to the* DS *terrace. The "fourth wall" of the drawing-room is a large patio window; all entrances to the terrace from the drawing-room are made through the side door*

Several pictures adorn the drawing-room walls and there are shelves of books. The furniture is comfortable if a little worn. There are a sofa, easy chairs and a coffee table with a letter lying on it. There is a sideboard with a drinks tray and glasses, phone and answering machine on it

The terrace extends R *around the side of the house and is edged with shrubs. A large swing seat with canopy stands* DR. *Because of the canopy, the occupants of the swing seat cannot be seen from the area of the drawing-room. There is an iron coffee table in front of the swing seat and a second table with chairs adjacent. An iron golf club is leaning against a chair*

When the CURTAIN *rises the electric lights are on in the drawing-room; the light fades from the terrace during the scene*

Nell stands by the sideboard, holding two drinks. She is slim, attractive and in her early forties

Gail, Nell's younger sister, enters from the hall. Gail is in her late twenties and is a plainer version of her sister. She is wearing a smart business suit. At the moment she is looking concerned

Gail What is it, Nell?
Nell You'll need a drink. I know *I* do.

Nell hands Gail a drink. They sit

Gail Well?
Nell First of all I don't want you telling anyone about this. I don't want Mother finding out, not yet.

Gail Finding out what?

Nell picks up the letter from the coffee table and hands it to Gail

Nell It's from John. He's left me.
Gail (*reading*) "Dear Nell, I can't take any more ..."
Nell He couldn't.
Gail (*continuing*) "I have to get away and sort myself out. I've left as much money as I can afford in the joint account". (*She pauses, staring at the letter. Reading*) "The cat's not been fed."
Nell (*drily*) Thoughtful to the end.

Gail reads the rest of the note in silence

Gail (*looking up*) I'm sorry, Nell.
Nell (*hopefully*) Did he say that?
Gail No, I did. There's no expression of regret here. (*She throws the note down*) The rat.
Nell Don't call him that. It's not his fault — it's all the worries of the last few months. I should have read the signs. He must have had some sort of brainstorm. He didn't know what he was doing, Gail.
Gail He remembered the cat.
Nell He was fond of the cat.
Gail Pity he wasn't as fond of you. Or have you been fed? Where do you think he's gone?
Nell I've no idea. Probably walking the streets somewhere. I daren't think, Gail. I daren't think where he's gone or what he might do...
Gail (*concerned*) You don't think ... ?
Nell We've been trading at a loss for over a year. We could paper these walls with writs — and yesterday I bought those shoes.
Gail Not the expensive ones?
Nell Yes. He just crumpled when he saw them. I've always been too extravagant.
Gail He didn't leave you because of a pair of shoes. He's always been short of money — it's never worried him before. Why now?
Nell Perhaps he was tired of trying to keep up appearances. I don't know.
Gail He was certainly keeping up appearances the other night. I've never seen him so cheerful.
Nell You couldn't see beyond the laughter, Gail. You couldn't see the pain. Besides, they say that when someone makes up his mind to do something — drastic — his mood lightens.
Gail (*alarmed*) My God! What are you going to do?
Nell Wait by the phone. He might ring. He's in such distress he's bound to have forgotten something. He hasn't packed a case in years.

Gail What did he take?

Nell Shirts, shoes, suits, socks, ties, overcoats — golf clubs.

Gail Golf clubs? Well, I can't see him walking the streets with that lot. And he doesn't seem to have forgotten much. Overcoats — he's providing for next winter. I don't think he'll ring.

Nell He'll ring because once he's had time to think he'll have second thoughts. He'll feel foolish and want to come back. That's why I have to carry on as if nothing's happened. That's why I don't want you to say anything — not even to Mother.

The doorbell rings

During the following, Helen enters round the rear of the house. She is in her late thirties, smartly dressed, with a little primness around the mouth. She looks into the drawing-room through the patio window

Gail He's back!

Nell That's Helen Rush. She was coming over to borrow a cookbook.

Gail But she's a terrible gab.

Nell I know.

Gail And nosy.

Nell Yes. I'm surprised she's not looking through the window.

Gail Perhaps she'll go away.

Nell She won't go away. (*She fetches a cookbook from a shelf*) Just remember nothing's happened.

Gail Suppose she mentions John?

Nell She won't. She never mentions John. They loathe each other. John plays snooker with George Rush every Tuesday night and she resents it. John's the last person she'd mention. (*She moves to the hall door*) I'll get rid of her...

Gail and Nell are suddenly aware that Helen is looking into the drawing-room. They all wave

Helen comes into the drawing-room by the side door

Helen I thought you may have been in the garden. (*She smiles at Gail*) Hallo, Gail. Still single?

Gail Hallo, Helen. Still married?

Helen But of course.

During the following line Nell gives Gail a stricken look

Gail No "of course" about it, Helen. One in three marriages ends in divorce and there's three of us here. I only have to get married and one of us could be in trouble ... (*Her voice dies away as she catches Nell's look. Hastily*) Is that the book? What are you cooking?

Nell (*holding the book out to Helen*) Here's the book, Helen. I've marked the place. I know you're in a hurry ...

Helen (*taking the book*) No hurry. (*She pauses for a moment and fixes Nell with a stare*) How's John?

Nell John?

Helen Yes, how is he?

Nell He's ... He's ... I ... er ... (*She falters and turns away*)

Helen Nell, what is it?

Gail (*whispering*) He's left.

Nell turns and frowns at Gail in annoyance

Helen (*knowingly*) Ah.

Nell What do you mean — "Ah"?

Helen Nothing.

Nell Helen, you can't say "Ah" like that and then say it's nothing. You weren't surprised, were you?

Helen No.

Gail What are you trying to say, Helen?

Helen I think Nell knows what I'm trying to say.

Nell No, I don't.

Helen I was trying to say — Barbara Buckley.

Gail Barbara Buckley?

Helen I think Nell understands.

Nell But I don't understand. Barbara Buckley's a customer. She's had trouble with her damp course.

Helen *Prolonged* trouble with her damp course according to George. Have you met her, Nell?

Nell No.

Helen Blonde, bold-looking woman with painted toe-nails.

Nell Bold. John would run a mile from a woman like that.

Helen He wasn't running from her last Tuesday. I saw them together.

Nell Not last Tuesday. John plays snooker with George every Tuesday. You know that.

Helen Not last Tuesday. I recognized him, Nell. And you can't mistake Barbara Buckley. She's a big woman.

Nell But John doesn't like big women. Everyone knows that.

Helen I saw them coming out of a restaurant. It was late.

Nell John doesn't eat late — it gives him indigestion. It must have been a trick of the light. What would he be doing with Barbara Buckley. Have you ever

known him show any interest in other women? Have you ever known him
make a pass? I mean, isn't it ridiculous … ?

*There is an uncomfortable silence; Nell realizes this. Helen and Gail look at
each other. During the following, Helen puts the cookbook on the table*

Well, someone say something.

Helen Nell, I never intended to mention this but there was — an incident at
your last party.

Nell Incident. What incident?

Helen I was cutting some extra sandwiches in the kitchen and John came in
and kissed me and said "You're a very attractive woman."

Nell (*staring*) He said that?

Helen Yes.

Gail Perhaps he was drunk.

*During the following, Gail picks up the cookbook and flicks through the
pages in an embarrassed manner*

Helen (*indignantly*) He wasn't drunk. Fortunately I had the bread knife in
my hand so it didn't go any further. But that's why I've been cool with him
ever since. You must have noticed, Nell, how we avoid each other.

Nell That's because he doesn't like you.

Helen What?

Nell He's never liked you. He must have been drunk. He must have mistaken
you for someone else — his mother.

Helen (*angrily*) He didn't mistake me for his mother.

Nell Helen, there were a number of women at that party — women he liked.
Why didn't he make a pass at them? Why not Gail for example? Really,
I can't believe all this … (*She sees Gail flicking through the cookery book
in an embarrassed manner*) What's the matter with you?

Gail Nothing.

Nell Don't you start. What is it?

Gail I remember that party only too well. I was sitting out there on the terrace
and John came out and put his hand on my knee and said "You get prettier
every day."

Nell Well, that's not true for a start. Can't you see that was being brotherly.
He's always been concerned about you — that you've never got married
and can't sustain a relationship.

Gail What about your relationship? (*She hesitates*) I saw him last Tuesday
night, as well.

Nell What?

Gail It was late. He was seeing this woman into a taxi…

Helen (*nodding*) Barbara Buckley.

Nell No!

Helen Nell, the truth is that John hasn't been playing snooker with George every Tuesday. He's been seeing Barbara Buckley. George has obviously been covering for him. I'm only sorry I was the one who had to tell you. But the sooner it's faced the better.

Gail Helen's right.

Helen (*smugly*) Of course I am.

Gail There's just one thing that puzzles me. If John has been seeing Barbara Buckley every Tuesday when he was supposed to be seeing George — who's George been seeing?

Helen looks disturbed for a moment. She frowns and takes the cookery book from Gail

Helen Well, thank you for the book, Nell. If there's anything I can do, you only have to ask. (*She moves to the hall door and turns*) How does one so young become so cynical?

Helen exits

Nell Well, you were a great help, I must say. Blabbermouth.

Gail She knew, Nell. She only came to rub it in.

We hear the sound of Helen's car departing

Nell (*sighing*) Everyone seems to have known but me. You, Helen, George Rush.

Gail They say the wife's usually the last to know.

Nell And I thought George Rush was my friend.

Gail Didn't you have any suspicions?

Nell No, in fact, John's been more attentive than ever lately.

Gail That's a sign.

Nell Is it?

Gail They get all fired up.

Nell Gail, where do you get all this stuff from? I thought I had a good marriage. Where did I go wrong?

Gail Don't start blaming yourself. That's what wives do in these situations. If he prefers Barbara Buckley ... (*She shakes her head*) He must be out of his mind.

Nell Why? What's she like?

Gail (*after a hesitation*) Well, if it's the woman I saw getting into a taxi ——

Nell Yes?

Gail She's not particularly attractive.

Nell You mean she's fat?

Gail Well, she's in proportion but ——

Nell But she's fat. He's left me for a tub of lard, hasn't he?

Gail Well, some men find that very attractive. They're highly prized in the East.

Nell We're not in the East. He's probably been waiting for someone like her all his life. He obviously wanted something to grab hold of. Probably couldn't believe his luck — probably leapt on her with a tape measure. (*She looks down at her figure*) I wonder how long it would take me to put on a few pounds?

Gail Why bother? Why have him back? What is he after all? A failed builder.

Nell I didn't marry him because I thought he was a genius. Anyway, I wouldn't say "failed".

Gail Nell, in the last high wind three of his walls collapsed.

Nell He's been cutting back on materials.

There is the sound of a car horn

Nell and Gail look at each other and dart to the window US

Gail Is it John?

Nell turns away from the window in disgust

Nell No, it's George Rush.

Gail What's he doing here?

Nell (*with a cold smile*) Can't you guess? It's Tuesday! Don't you see? John hasn't told him. It must have been a last-minute decision. George is here to pick him up for snooker. Only we know it's not snooker, don't we? It's another game those two have been playing.

Gail (*peering out of the window*) The rat. I never knew what John saw in him.

Nell No, I never thought they had anything in common — until now. He used to teach Christopher. God knows what he taught him. John and I met him at the PTA meetings. He writes poetry.

Gail Poetry. You can't trust poets — their minds are too active.

Nell You obviously can't trust George Rush.

Gail (*returning to the room from the window*) He's coming to the door.

Nell Right. Would you mind going out the back, Gail? I'd prefer to see him alone. (*She heads for the door* US)

Gail (*grimly*) Don't worry — I don't want to meet him. But he'll remember me.

Nell turns back from the hall door, looking worried

Nell What do you mean?
Gail Anyone who crosses my sister — crosses me.

Nell exits into the hall looking even more worried

Gail moves through the side door on to the terrace. She glances around, picks up the golf club from by the chair and exits through the garden L

Nell enters from the hall followed by George Rush. George is a little younger than Nell. His hair is curly and unkempt and his suit is slightly rumpled

Nell (*silkily*) Come in, George. Sit down.
George (*sitting*) John not here then?
Nell Not at the moment.
George Not like him to be late.
Nell No, but people do sometimes surprise you, don't they?
George (*uncertainly*) Er, yes … (*He watches her cautiously during the following*)
Nell Let me get you a drink. Gin and tonic, isn't it?
George Thank you.
Nell (*pouring a gin and tonic*) I know John really looks forward to these evenings.
George Does he?
Nell Oh, yes. The sight of the green baize, the feel of the cue, the click of the balls — it's music to him. (*She hands George his drink*) Some nights he can hardly wait. How's the drink?

George sips his drink

George Fine.
Nell How long is it since you two started playing, George?
George About three months, I think.
Nell Three months. And is he improving?
George What?
Nell Is he improving?
George His potting's much better.
Nell So I understand.
George But he still has trouble with snookers.
Nell I wouldn't be too sure about that, George. He may have snookered you tonight …

George What?

There is the sound of shattering glass. George rises hastily and moves to the UC *window, followed by Nell*

George It's your sister!
Nell Yes.
George She's just smashed my headlight!
Nell She always was impulsive. Never mind, you still have the other one.

There is a second crash

Nell Well, you did have.

George moves towards the the hall door, then stops

George What am I supposed to do now?
Nell Get home before lighting-up time.

There is the sound of the car driving away from the house. George watches it go from the window

George Your sister's insane.
Nell At least she's done something positive. I wish I had. I wish I could say that drink was poisoned and you only had half an hour to live.

George sighs and returns to his chair

George You know, don't you?
Nell About Barbara Buckley? Big woman — all meat and potatoes? Yes. Your wife told me. You've just missed her. (*She pauses*) How could you, George?
George He asked me for help. He was desperate.
Nell Desperate! Look at me. I'm desperate. So he asked you for help. Well, I know there's such a thing as friendship but what about me? I thought I was your friend too.
George You are.
Nell And what about Christopher and Ellie? What am I going to tell them when they come home? Did you give them a thought? No, because you were too busy messing around. I hate you, George Rush.
George I didn't encourage him, Nell. I was trying to prevent him doing something drastic. I thought he'd grow tired of her.
Nell No, he grew tired of me, George. And he has done something drastic. He's left me.

George Oh.

Nell Yes — "Oh". And is Barbara Buckley married?

George Yes.

Nell And what did she tell her husband about Tuesday nights?

George Netball.

Nell Netball! And he believed her. How could anyone so elephantine play netball?

George She's not elephantine exactly ——

Nell She's fat. I've heard how fat she is.

George She wasn't always like that. (*He pauses*) She's pregnant.

Nell (*sitting*) Pregnant?

George Yes.

Nell (*quietly*) She's quite young, then? Only I didn't think she was ...

George Oh yes. (*He pauses*) I suppose that's why they went away. I'm sorry. I suppose you think I'm a louse.

Nell (*rising*) No. I've nothing against lice. They leave me alone — I leave them alone. No, if I was going to compare you to an insect it would be a dung beetle because you've come here with a load of crap, George. All this about being my friend and not wanting this to happen. (*She moves and opens the hall door for him to leave*)

George moves towards the door but stops by it

George You're right, Nell. It was a load of crap.

Nell (*staring*) What?

George I did want this to happen. (*He closes the door*)

Nell You wanted it to happen? My God! Why? You must really hate me.

George No. I love you.

Nell What was that?

George I love you.

Nell backs away

George (*following Nell*) I've always loved you — from the first time I saw you. That parents' evening when you came to talk about Christopher. You looked so beautiful and assured and yet strangely vulnerable.

Nell I always look vulnerable when I talk about Christopher.

George Don't laugh, Nell. I mean every word. And when John said he loved Barbara ——

Nell He actually said that?

George Yes. It was then I began to think there was a chance. I wasn't seeing anyone when John was seeing Barbara. I spent my nights drinking and thinking about you. (*He moves towards Nell*)

Nell (*moving away towards the telephone*) You're married, George.

George So are you. So is John. So is Barbara Buckley. What does it mean?
Nell What does it mean to Helen?
George She doesn't even like me.
Nell You have three children, George. She must have liked you a little.
George That was in the past. It was before I met you.
Nell George, I'm sorry your wife doesn't like you but what makes you think I will?
George Just give me a chance, Nell.
Nell But what about the children? Muffin — Puffin — and what's the other one?
George Pumpkin.
Nell Pumpkin. What about them?
George They don't like me either.
Nell No-one seems to like you, George. Do you think it might be something to do with your personality?

George corners her by the telephone

George I just want to feel your warmth, Nell …
Nell You're not feeling my warmth, George.
George (*looking deep into her eyes*) I could drown in your eyes, Nell.
Nell (*staring*) What?
George (*putting his arms around Nell's waist and sinking to his knees*) Oh, Nell…

Nell stares down in astonishment. The phone begins to ring. She struggles to answer it with George still clinging to her waist

Nell (*into the phone*) Hallo?... Oh, it's you, Gail. If you're using your mobile on the motorway get both hands on the wheel. I've told you about that before — it's dangerous. … Yes, I'm all right. (*She glances down at George*) It's amazing how you can adapt. … No, I'm not feeling sorry for myself — and I don't feel rejected. Quite the contrary. … What? Oh, yes — I really told him. … Yes, you did make a lovely job of his headlights. … No, I'm sure he won't sue. Gail, I've got to go — I've got something cooking. I think it's burning. Bye. (*She replaces the phone and glares down at George*)

George slowly removes his hands and returns humbly to his chair. He and Nell regard each other in silence

Nell (*after a pause*) What was that about my eyes?

CURTAIN

SCENE 2

The same. Summer. Afternoon

It is hot. There is a jug of lemonade on the table and some glasses

When the CURTAIN *rises, Nell is sitting on the swing seat. She is wearing a crisp white shirt and a skirt*

George enters through garden from L. *He is carrying a battered briefcase. He puts his head around the canopy*

George (*in a sinister tone*) Excuse me, madam. I've come to look at the house.
Nell (*taking on his manner*) It is by appointment.
George I acted on impulse. I am an impulsive man.
Nell Really?
George I hope I'm not disturbing you. Only I see there's more than one glass.
Nell No, I'm quite alone. But you never know who's going to drop in, do you? Would you care for some lemonade?
George You're very kind — the heat is intense, is it not?

Nell pours George some lemonade; he sips it

George So you're quite alone, not expecting anyone; no member of the family returning?
Nell My children are at college.
George And your husband?
Nell He's no longer with us.
George Dead?
Nell Surbiton.
George Almost the same thing. (*He sits by Nell and runs his fingers over the back of the seat*)
George Do you think I could see the master bedroom?
Nell Isn't that rather unusual?
George I'm an unusual man.
Nell One normally starts downstairs.
George I don't.
Nell Perhaps the garden first ...
George The garden ... (*He looks around and slowly his manner changes*) I've never done it in a garden before, Nell. (*He removes his jacket and loosens his tie*) You don't think we'll frighten the squirrels?
Nell Well, if they start dropping out of the trees we'll stop.

George (*unbuttoning his shirt*) Nice to feel the sun dappling our skins, Nell. I just feel like a little dappling. (*He looks around cautiously*) Sure we won't be disturbed?

Nell Quite sure.

George I left my car down in the village.

George kisses Nell

You know I shall miss this place when you sell it.

Nell (*staring*) Who said I was selling?

George There's a board up at the end of the lane.

Nell straightens in astonishment

Nell I thought you were joking. I didn't have it put there.

George Oh. Probably kids. I thought you'd finally made up your mind.

Nell No. A "For Sale" board?

George Yes. You'd better get it moved. We don't want people calling.

Nell (*wryly*) Of course not. That wouldn't do at all.

George glances at his watch

(*Sharply*) Don't look at your watch!

George Sorry.

Nell How long have you got?

George I'm supposed to be giving an extra hour's tuition.

Nell Oh dear. It's going to be a quickie, isn't it? (*She breaks away and moves across the terrace*)

George (*wincing*) Don't say that, Nell.

Nell You said you could manage most of the evening.

George I thought I could.

Nell You said Helen was going to her mother's.

George She is. But she can't take the girls. Apparently there's a concert and they haven't got their bunnies' ears.

Nell Their what?

George Bunnies' ears. I have to pick them up. Then I have to take Dad to the surgery — another fall I'm afraid. And then if I've got time I have to take the dog to the vet's.

Nell (*staring*) What dog?

George What?

Nell What dog, George?

George We've got a dog. Didn't I tell you?

Nell No, you didn't.

George The girls wanted a dog. They've called it Buttons. Do you know why?

Nell I'm not interested in why they call it Buttons. Haven't you got enough
responsibilities? A wife, an aged father, three daughters, Muffin, Puffin
and Stuffin.

George Pumpkin.

Nell And now you've got a dog called Buttons. I can just see you all running
through the park in your matching sweaters, Helen holding your hand, the
children on your shoulders, Buttons leaping about you — and all of you
looking like an advert for life insurance.

George We don't wear matching sweaters.

Nell You do surprise me. I've never known anyone more married than you,
George. And now your father's falling down. Do you realize that by the
time your children are old enough to be told about us, your father will be
too fragile to stand the shock.

George You're not thinking, Nell. The dog could be useful.

Nell Could it?

George Dogs have to be walked…

Nell You're not bringing it here. I've got a cat.

George He could sit in the car. And dogs can't talk.

Nell Then why make him sit in the car? He could come in and watch.

George What's the matter with you today? Have you heard from John?

Nell No, and I don't want to. I want to forget him.

George Then why do you still wear his wedding ring?

Nell Status. It helps me get a better cut of meat at the butcher's.

George glances at his watch. Nell glares

George Well, are we going to or not?

Nell What, George?

George Lock limbs — have knowledge of each other?

Nell (*studying George*) Do you mean make love? I notice you never say
make love these days. Why is that?

George (*sighing*) Because if I say make love — the word love is used. Then
you say "If you love me, why don't you do something about it?"

Nell Why don't you?

George You see — we're there already.

George kisses Nell

Nell Sometimes I think this is all you come for — this and to play silly games.

George On the contrary, it's not all I come for. I've brought you this. (*He
fishes in his briefcase, takes out a slim volume and waves it triumphantly*)
I'd almost forgotten.

Nell (*excitedly*) The poems?

George Out today—and in all self-respecting bookshops. Read those words and say I don't love you.

Nell takes the book and flicks through it. She pauses at the front

What are you looking for?
Nell Nothing. It's beautifully laid out. Read one.

George takes the book from Nell

George You know I don't like reading my own poems.
Nell You mean you don't like reading them to me. Is it because the word love might be used?
George How can you say that?

George draws Nell back to the swing seat

This book wouldn't have been written without you. I'm a better poet because of you, Nell. You run through my work like a golden thread …
Nell (*softening*) A golden thread …

They kiss

You certainly have a way with words, George. (*She pours more lemonade*)

George darts a quick glance at his watch. He removes his trousers during the following

Nell (*turning in mock surprise*) Mr Rush! You're removing your trousers.
George You've noticed that …
Nell I couldn't help it.
George I thought it might arouse your interest.
Nell It's certainly a talking point …

George lays his trousers neatly beside him. They embrace

Jim Grant enters the garden R. He is in his late fifties, handsome, and rather distinguished. He is carrying a jacket over one arm and is holding a brochure. He passes by the back of the swing seat, looking thoughtfully at the house

Nell and George become aware of Jim's presence. Nell looks round the canopy. George crouches frantically. Nell puts a calming hand on George, straightens her clothes and moves to meet Jim who is still looking at the house

Jim (*turning; businesslike*) Ah, you're here.
Nell (*mystified*) Yes. (*She moves across Jim to draw his gaze from the swing seat*)
Jim My name's Grant. Jim Grant. I made an appointment. They said there'd be someone here to meet me.
Nell Did they?

Nell draws Jim further towards the house

George slowly pulls down the canopy until only his legs are visible. He then raises his legs under the canopy until he has vanished entirely. During the follwing, he tries to get his trousers back on — but it is a struggle

Jim (*looking down the garden*) Nice garden.
Nell Yes.
Jim I could live here.
Nell Could you?
Jim I've studied the brochure.
Nell (*staring*) Brochure?
Jim It's well within my range.
Nell You have a brochure?
Jim Yes. Picked it up at your office.

Jim hands Nell the brochure and peers into the drawing-room. Nell studies the brochure in bewilderment

I think the price is reasonable but then I understand they need a quick sale. I believe they're in trouble at the bank.
Nell Is that what you heard?
Jim I don't know much about them. I live on the other side of the village. I'd heard they'd done a bunk. (*He regards Nell curiously for a moment*) Aren't you going to show me round?
Nell Er, why don't you just browse — and ask me questions afterwards? That way you won't feel hurried …
Jim If that's all right.
Nell Perfectly.

Jim goes into the drawing-room through the side door. Nell watches him through the window. They smile at each other. He straightens a picture

(*Returning to the swing seat; hissing*) John's put the house up. He's had brochures printed. How could he have done all that without me knowing?
George (*from behind the canopy*) Probably waited until you were away on the school trip — it would only take a day.

Nell I didn't know he'd put the house up as security.

George You must have signed the papers.

Nell (*desperately*) I signed a lot of things — I was a director. Of all the ——

George Keep your voice down. I'm not supposed to be here.

Nell Neither am I apparently. I'm supposed to have done a bunk. (*She moves back to the dining-room window*)

Jim exits into the hall

Nell sees Jim leave and returns to the swing seat, raising the canopy. George is still struggling into his trousers

What am I going to do?

George Well, if there's anything left you'll get a proportion.

Nell I don't want a proportion. This is my house.

George Sounds as if it's the bank's.

Nell Do you know why I've always liked this house? Because he didn't build it. And now he sneaks back and does this. How could he?

George They can't just turn you out. Go to a solicitor.

Nell I must say, you're very calm about it.

George Calm? I'm trying to get into these bloody trousers. Anyway, houses don't sell overnight.

Nell This one will. It's just what he's looking for.

George Then you'll have to put him off. Pass me my jacket. And get rid of him. I'll ring you from the call box.

There is the sound of a garden gate opening. George retreats behind the canopy

Gail enters the garden L

Gail I didn't know you'd put the house up.

Nell What?

Gail I didn't know the house was up for sale.

Nell (*moving hastily to meet Gail*) Neither did I. John did it.

Nell leads Gail into the drawing-room

Gail The rat. (*She makes to sit down*)

Nell I'm busy, Gail. I have a man looking over the house.

Gail does not sit down

Gail Then I should stay.

Nell He's perfectly respectable.

Gail When a woman's on her own, no man's respectable. And you're not busy—you've been sunbathing, I can smell the Ambre Solaire. You're not living in the real world, Nell. You won't meet a man this way.

Nell (*innocently*) Won't I?

Gail And what are you going to do about the house?

Nell Sell it apparently. I certainly can't keep up the payments.

Gail So you sit around here getting further and further into debt and doing nothing.

Nell I'm not trained for anything, Gail.

Gail You've worked in an office.

Nell That was years ago. The adding machines had handles in those days. Since then I've been mixing concrete for my husband—driving a lorry and raising two children. And what have I got to show for it? Writs.

Gail Well, I've done something about it. I've got you an interview for a job at our place.

Nell But I don't know anything about insurance.

Gail Look, most of them don't know anything about insurance but it doesn't stop them working there. And it's not difficult. It's in Terry's section. A little typing, reception, records. It's a nice job.

Nell If it's a nice job there'll be competition.

Gail No, there won't, because you'll be the first and only applicant. Even Terry doesn't know she's left. I found her sobbing in the Ladies.

Nell (*nervously*) Sobbing? Why was she sobbing?

Gail She said she couldn't take any more.

Nell I don't like the sound of this, Gail. What couldn't she take any more?

Gail It's nothing to worry about. She was too young.

Nell Well, I should be all right there.

Gail And they say he hates women.

Nell Well, I'm not too keen on them myself but won't that be a drawback?

Gail No, because I don't believe it. Terry's bark's much worse than his bite.

Nell I'm not worried about the bite at the moment, what's his bark like? I mean, will I get Christmas Day off?

Gail He's not a Scrooge. It's just that he has this cynical attitude towards women. His wife left him.

Nell What! You're not trying to fix me up again, are you, Gail? He's not going to leap on top of me from the filing cabinet?

Gail No. Terry's only interested in work. And it's not as if you don't know how to handle men.

Nell Oh yes. I handled one so well he disappeared without leaving a forwarding address.

Gail You mustn't let that undermine you, Nell. You're mature, sophisticated and attractive.

Nell (*after a pause*) Keep talking.

Gail You're an interesting and amusing companion. And what's more you make a man feel interesting and amusing. I've noticed that.

Nell Gail, you don't think that the fact that you're my sister might prejudice you a little?

The sound of heavy footsteps comes from upstairs

What's he doing up there? I think he's jumping up and down on the floorboards! (*She moves to the hall door*)

Gail drifts out on to the terrace to get a drink

George chooses this moment to leave the swing seat and disappear through the garden R

Gail Good heavens! (*She crosses the terrace and stares after George*)

Nell (*joining Gail; anxiously*) What's the matter?

Gail I've just seen George Rush.

Nell (*vaguely*) George…?

Gail Rush. He's creeping about your garden. Look.

They both stare down the garden

You can just see him crouching behind that bush.

Nell Oh, yes.

Gail What's he doing?

Nell Weeding. People have been so kind since John left.

Gail He's not weeding. He's hiding. He obviously thinks he can't be seen from here.

Nell He always was an optimist.

Gail Now he's scurrying off. (*She turns suspiciously on Nell*) What's going on, Nell? What have you been doing?

Nell (*sighing*) I think it's what's known as messing around.

Gail Nell, he's married.

Nell She nags him.

Gail He also has three little girls.

Nell They nag him as well. And now he's got a dog called Buttons. It won't be long before it's snapping at his heels.

Gail You can't do this, Nell.

Nell It was done to me.

Gail And you know how you felt.

Nell Yes, and no-one gave a damn.

Gail How often does he come here?

Nell Now and then.

Gail Nell, there's no future in going with someone who's married to someone else.

Nell Gail, there was no future in it when I was going with someone who was married to me.

Gail How far have things gone?

Nell What?

Gail Has the worst happened?

Nell (*indignantly*) What do you mean — the worst?

Gail You know what I mean. How far, Nell?

Nell (*hesitantly*) Well, if we were making for London. London being the worst that could happen — we're somewhere near Watford.

Gail (*studying Nell closely*) You're fibbing.

Nell All right. Marble Arch.

Gail Oh, my God!

Nell He's getting a divorce.

Gail He can't afford a divorce. He's a teacher. Nell, what have I said about the real world?

Nell I'm not living in it.

Gail Right. The interview's tomorrow morning. Wear that dark suit, the one you wear when you meet your creditors — you'll need all the help you can get …

Gail exits L *through the garden*

Nell returns to the drawing-room and pours herself a vodka and tonic

Jim enters from the hall. He regards Nell for a moment.

Jim Should you be doing that?

Nell What?

Jim Drinking their vodka?

Nell It's one of the perks.

Jim Oh. They certainly left in a hurry. The deep freeze is almost full.

Nell (*mournfully*) It won't last.

Jim (*glances at glass*) No. I imagine not. (*He studies Nell*) Have we met before?

Nell No. Are you going to buy it?

Jim I think so.

Nell I wouldn't.

Jim What? Aren't you supposed to be selling it?

Nell Only after a full and frank disclosure.

Jim What disclosure?

Nell Why do you think they left in such a hurry? Drinks on the sideboard — food in the deep freeze.

Jim I thought they were in debt.

Nell No, they found out about the tragedy.

Jim What tragedy?

Nell Previous owners. He was messing around and she found out. She went insane with a pair of garden shears.

Jim I've never heard about that.

Nell It was kept quiet.

Jim But I only live on the other side of the village.

Nell It may as well be the moon. They're very different on this side …

Jim Are they?

Nell Inbreeding. She waited until he was in a drunken stupor and took her revenge. She began snipping things off him.

Jim I can hardly believe it.

Nell Neither could the police. They'd never seen anything like it. Two of them resigned the force. She tried to hide the remains but the secret drove her mad. She never knew when parts of him were going to turn up. Eventually she drowned herself in the river. But they say her ghost still haunts the terrace.

Jim I don't believe in ghosts — only flesh and blood.

Nell They're still finding it; they found a finger in a pickle jar only recently.

Jim smiles at her

(*Seeing the smile*) Don't you believe me?

Jim I might have done but I suddenly remembered where I'd seen you before. In the photograph by your bed. It's your house, isn't it?

Nell Yes.

Jim I'm sorry. But I'm sure you'll share in what's left.

Nell There won't be anything left.

Jim Are the debts considerable?

Nell Are you serious? My husband, the loony builder. If they hadn't built the Leaning Tower of Pisa, that would have been his next project. I love this house.

Jim I loved my house but in the end we have to remind ourselves — it's only bricks and mortar.

Nell But that's what I love about it. You can depend on bricks and mortar. It's always there in the evening — not out pretending to play snooker.

Jim Ah, now I see. Your husband's left you.

Nell (*sarcastically*) My God! Does it show?

Jim I'm sorry. I know what it's like to be suddenly alone. I was widowed last year.

Nell Oh, now I'm sorry.

Jim I can't live there any more … Too many memories —— (*He turns away from Nell*)

Nell watches Jim curiously. He moves to the wall and slowly and carefully straightens a picture

Nell Can I get you a drink — er — Jim?

Jim Well, I've had a few at lunchtime but perhaps a small gin and tonic — er ——

Nell Nell. (*She pours the drink during the following*)

Jim Nell. I find I'm doing more of that these days — since it happened … (*His eye is taken by another picture. He straightens it*) It helps, I suppose …

Nell Was it very sudden? (*She holds the drink out to him*)

Jim Yes. She was washed off the sea front at Ramsgate.

Nell (*stopping in the act of passing the drink*) My goodness! That is sudden.

Jim One moment by my side — the next moment gone. First holiday in years.

Nell That must have been awful. I didn't realize the sea could be so rough at Ramsgate.

Jim It was out of season. I was always too busy. Worst storms for twenty years — driftwood as far back as the railway station. The emergency services were magnificent but to no avail. I blame myself. (*He takes the drink and turns away, obviously under deep emotional strain*)

Nell (*patting him gently on the shoulder*) You mustn't do that.

Jim That's what they tell me. I gave her the most magnificent funeral. Everyone came. I didn't realize she had so many friends …

Nell That must have been a comfort.

Jim We often talked about what we'd do if the other one died. But I always felt she thought it would be me. I was older. That's why I wasn't sure if she meant it when she said I should marry again. What do you think?

Nell I don't think I'd want my husband to marry again if I died. I think I'd prefer a period of grief followed by a spectacular suicide.

Jim (*regarding Nell doubtfully*) There have been a approaches from one or two ladies in the village. Delivery of pies, pastries, home-made jam. All fairly harmless.

Nell (*smiling*) Well, you're safe here, Jim — I'm right out of home -made jam.

Jim You know, you're a very unusual woman. How could he have walked out on you?

Nell He just put one foot in front of the other. You'd be surprised how easy it is.

Jim (*sighing*) Nothing would surprise me any more, Nell. You see, after I got back from the funeral I found some letters in her wardrobe. They were from several men. They were very graphic. I always thought she played golf in the afternoons.

Nell (*knowingly*) But she didn't?

Jim No. (*He turns and gropes for his handkerchief*) I'm sorry. It was such a shock…

Nell watches Jim in embarrassment. She puts an awkward hand on his shoulder

Nell (*lightly*) Now, Jim — if this is a way of getting me to lower the price — it's not going to work.

To Nell's surprise, Jim turns and buries his head on her shoulder and begins to sob softly. The phone rings. Struggling, with one arm around Jim, Nell answers the phone

(*Into the phone*) Sorry. There's something boiling over. …I'll ring you back later. (*She replaces the phone and pats Jim awkwardly on the shoulder, continuing to do so as the scene closes*)

CURTAIN

SCENE 3

The same. Night. A week later

When the CURTAIN *rises, the house and terrace are in darkness. There is a copy of George's book on the sideboard*

The Lights in the drawing-room come on abruptly

Nell enters. She throws down her handbag and coat. George follows, looking apologetic

Nell That was a disaster.

George I'm sorry, Nell.

Nell We travel thirty miles for a quiet dinner — our first for a month — and it was an unmitigated disaster.

George It wasn't my fault.

Nell Then whose fault was it?

George I'm a teacher, Nell. I've taught hundreds of boys. I never know when I'm going to bump into one.

Nell Who do you think you are — Mr Chips?

George Hardly Mr Chips. Did you see the way he was glaring? Why do they hate me so? I only taught them English.

Nell They don't hate you.

George They do. I passed an old boy in the street last week. He muttered, "Rush, you bastard", and spat in the gutter.

Nell So we spent the rest of the evening hiding and hardly daring to talk. I don't know why we didn't sit at separate tables and pass notes to each other — it would have been easier.

George Oh, I don't know. You didn't seem to suffer from any restraint.

Nell What do you mean?

George Well, as rows go I thought it was one of our best. We could have sold tickets. The whole restaurant was listening.

Nell No, they weren't.

George They stopped eating, Nell. They stilled their cutlery. They wouldn't even chew in case they missed a word. I saw them shushing each other.

Nell Don't be ridiculous.

George And don't think I didn't notice the artificially raised voice — raised to cause me maximum embarrassment.

Nell You're easily embarrassed, George.

George You called me a worm.

Nell You are a worm.

George You see! The man who sat with his back to us couldn't wait to see what you looked like. He went to the Gents twice just to get a good look at you. So much for a discreet dinner. We did nothing but quarrel.

Nell They probably thought we were married.

George Married people don't talk to each other like that.

Nell You should know.

George I never realized how much you hated me.

Nell I don't hate you — that's the trouble.

George It was like looking into a snake pit. You were hissing and twitching.

Nell I wasn't hissing and twitching.

George Hissing and twitching. I don't think you even like me.

Nell I never said I liked you.

George You see!

Nell I said I loved you.

George (*doubtfully*) Do you?

Nell If I don't what's this all been for? (*She pauses*) Papers for the divorce came through today.

George I'm, sorry, Nell.

Nell I thought you'd be pleased. I'm going to be a free woman. So what are you going to do about it?

George You don't understand. I have to be careful. I'm a teacher. I deal with young minds. I'm coming up for head of department. And the governors are seriously religious.

Nell Oh. What is it, George? Do you think we may be setting a bad example?

George Well, I'm not exactly proud of myself.

Nell (*sharply*) What was that?

George I'm not exactly proud of myself.

Nell You're not exactly proud of me either, are you?

George It has nothing to do with you. You don't know what I'm going through. (*Pause*) They asked me to read the lesson on Founder's Day. I couldn't do it.

Nell Why not?

George It would have been hypocritical.

Nell studies George

Nell Do you think you've fallen from grace, George? Is that it? What are you going to do about it? Have me shrived?

George It doesn't matter.

Nell No, tell me. I'm seeing you in a new light. I didn't realize you had a calling.

George I didn't say I had a calling. I enjoyed reading the lesson, that's all.

Nell Yes, I once heard you reading the lesson when Chris was in the choir. I thought you sounded pompous.

George Pompous! Anyone who knows me could never call me pompous.

Nell I know you and I'm calling you pompous. What is it, George? Do you want to be respectable again? Do you want to dump me?

George No.

Nell Then why this sudden concern for the pupils? It was hardly evident on the school trip last month. Do you remember that night on the ferry? When you were beating on my cabin door because you wanted to have me in the middle of the North Sea in a force eight gale just for the hell of it. Apart from it being no way to treat a member of the PTA — the children could have been plummeting from the bridge for all you cared.

George Don't remind me.

Nell Don't you want to be reminded? Are you ashamed of what you've done? Because I'm not.

George It's not your fault, Nell — it's mine.

Nell Don't take responsibility for me.

George (*frowning*) What is the matter with you tonight?

Nell (*after a pause*) Jim came by at lunchtime.

George Jim?

Nell The man who wants to buy the house. He took me down to the pub.

George Good. You don't get out enough.

Nell You're not jealous?

George (*smiling*) Well, he's pretty ancient, isn't he?

Nell He's quite well-preserved.

George So are the Elgin Marbles but you wouldn't want to spend the night with them. (*Pause*) Did you enjoy yourself?

Nell Yes. He introduced me to his friends, that was a novelty.

George Well, he's free. (*He glances at his watch*) I'm married.

Nell How can I forget. You can always tell a married man. He's forever gazing at his watch.

George (*impatiently*) Well, are we going to or not?

Nell You mean, make love?

George Yes.

Nell Then say it, George.

George Are we going to make love?

Nell No.

George Right. (*He reaches for his coat and then stops*) Didn't you say he was a widower?

Nell Yes.

George He hasn't mourned for very long, has he?

Nell How long would you mourn? In the event of an unknown hand pushing Helen off Beachy Head?

George I don't know — I've never thought about it.

Nell You'd probably sit by her grave like a faithful hound — you and Buttons, howling in unison.

George What happened to his wife?

Nell She was swept off the sea front at Ramsgate.

George That's unusual.

Nell Unusual. It was a tragedy.

George Well, of course. (*Pause*) Was she well insured?

Nell Well insured! That's a terrible thing to say.

George Didn't you say he was an accountant?

Nell Yes.

George She'd be well insured.

Nell Why this obsession with insurance?

George I've never heard of anyone being swept off the sea front at Ramsgate.

Nell Well, you have now. And he's never got over it.

George He seems to be getting over it at the moment. (*Pause*) I suppose he's got plenty of money.

Nell I believe so.

George An accountant. I know the sort. Into money but no idea of the finer things of life.

Nell Don't be superior, George. Anyone who has fluffy lavatory seat covers, a Dralon three piece suite and eats onion bhajis from Marks can hardly lay claim to the higher things.

George I didn't realize that when you came to my house you looked at everything with such a jaundiced eye.

Nell Well, I must admit I was almost overwhelmed by the warm domestic atmosphere but I recovered.

George What has got into you tonight?

Nell Nothing.

George (*after a pause*) I suppose the money would be an advantage.

Nell George, I'm in debt, I'm losing my house — of course it would be an advantage.

George But you've got a job now.

Nell But for how long? I damaged the word processor today, yesterday I broke the photocopier, and I've done something to the fax machine. I'm going through that office like Genghis Khan. Besides, it doesn't pay that much. But that's not why I went to the pub with him.

George Are you sure? Money's a great aphrodisiac, Nell.

Nell How would you know?

George Has he mentioned me at all?

Nell Yes, he has, as a matter of fact. He couldn't understand why there wasn't a man in my life.

George You didn't tell him?

Nell No. But he wanted to know why your car was always in the lane. Why you visited so often.

George What did you tell him?

Nell I said you were a family friend. He'd heard of you.

George Had he?

Nell In fact, he bought your book.

Nell takes a book from the sideboard and hands it to George

(*Smiling cynically*) He wants you to autograph it. He thinks you're a celebrity.

George (*beaming*) Does he?

Nell (*drily*) I thought that would change your opinion of him.

George (*opening the book*) Where does he want me to sign?

Nell On the page where it says, "To Helen".

They regard each other in silence

George So that's it — that's what this is all about.

Nell I see there's no mention of the golden thread. But then in my book there's no mention of "To Helen". Apparently the page in my book had been cunningly removed. Why, George?

George I knew you'd be angry?
Nell I mean, why, "To Helen"?
George It was expected.
Nell Was it? Is she a golden thread too?
George Some of those poems were written before I knew you.
Nell Did you write them about her?
George I suppose so — I don't know.
Nell And did you say them to her when you made love? I presume you did make love or where did Muffin, Puffin and Rhubarb come from? They didn't arrive with the milk, did they?
George It was a long time ago.
Nell Yes, but what happens now? Do you write poems to both of us? Do you make love to both of us?
George Don't start that again.
Nell Only I couldn't help noticing on my brief visit to Chez Rush the rather cosy double bed.
George We have to keep up appearances, Nell.
Nell You mean for the sake of Muffin, Puffin and Gumdrop.
George Pumpkin. Why can't you use their proper names?
Nell Why can't you?

They stand glaring at each other. George makes to throw the book down but stops himself

George (*frowning*) Why did he want me to sign this particular page?
Nell It was at the front.
George It was almost as if he wanted to point out the dedication to you. Don't you think that's a little sinister?
Nell No. He merely wanted your autograph.
George It's as if he wanted to come between us.
Nell Well, that wouldn't be difficult, would it?
George (*starting*) What was that? Was that a car? I saw a light in the lane.
Nell Probably the neighbours.
George It's getting late. I'd better go. (*He moves to kiss Nell*)

Nell moves away. George moves to the door

Nell (*following George*) Here's a test for you, George. It's to prove you're a loyal and devoted lover. You're saying good-night to your mistress when the next door neighbour appears. Do you: (a) passionately kiss her good-night; (b) peck her politely on the cheek; (c) surreptitiously squeeze her hand; or (d) leap into the hedge? (*Pause*) We both know what you'd do, don't we?

George I have to go.

Nell You don't have to go. I want you to stay the night.

George What! I'm at an NUT branch meeting. We haven't had an all-night sitting in our history. What would Helen say?

Nell (*picking up the phone*) Why don't you ask her?

George What?

Nell Ring her. Tell her where you are. Do something positive for a change.

George Put that down.

Nell Should I ring her?

George No.

Nell (*dialling*) Should I tell her where you are?

George If you don't put that phone down I'll rip it from the wall.

Nell (*quietly*) Well, that was positive enough. I think I've finally got through to you. (*She replaces the phone*) I wouldn't have done it.

George Wouldn't you?

Nell I think you'd better go. (*She moves to her handbag and takes a bottle of tablets out of it*)

George (*hesitates*) What are you going to do?

Nell I'm going to take these tablets.

George Are they strong?

Nell Very. (*She pops some tablets into her mouth*)

George You shouldn't take too many.

Nell I want to sleep for a long time.

George Don't be silly, Nell. You've still got me.

Nell I'd sooner take the tablets.

The phone rings

George (*starting*) Now the phone's ringing.

Nell You answer it. I'm killing myself.

George examines the bottle of tablets

George No, you're not — these are sweeteners.

Nell I'm going to sweeten myself first.

George I can't answer it — not at this time of night.

Nell Don't get your knickers in a twist, George. There's always the answering machine.

The answering machine cuts in

Nell (*voice-over*) Hallo. Don't ring off. I'm not in at the moment but if you leave your name and number after the tone I'll get back to you. Bye.

Nell You see.

The tone sounds

Jim (*voice-over*) Hallo. It's Jim. You have a lovely voice, Nell.
George (*alarmed*) My God! Can he hear us?
Nell Of course not.
Jim (*voice-over*) I know it's late but I just wanted to say how much I enjoyed this lunchtime. All my friends were talking about you ——
George What did you do?
Nell A striptease.
Jim (*voice-over*) I was so proud of you — dear.
George Dear?
Jim (*voice-over*) Do you know where I am at the moment? In my car — in the bottom lane — looking at your lights.
George Oh, my God! (*He moves abruptly away from the window*)
Jim (*voice-over*) I started to worry about you living here alone. So I got in the car and came over. By the way I've brought that hose attachment.
George Hose attachment?
Jim (*voice-over*) But you may be tired. I'll wait a few moments — if the lights are still on I'll call. Bye — dear.

There is the sound of Jim ringing off

George switches off the lights

Nell Don't do that. (*She switches the lights back on*)
George He'll call.
Nell He's only bringing a hose attachment …
George Suppose he finds me here?
Nell Well, you haven't got "adulterer" branded on your forehead, George. You're a friend. You've a perfect right to be here. Try not to appear so ruffled. (*She sighs*) You look like a pigeon that's just flown into the double glazing. (*She moves to the hall door*)
George (*anxiously*) Where are you going?
Nell I'm going to freshen up. I have a visitor, George.

Nell exits into the hall

George groans. He dims the drawing-room lights and creeps cautiously on to the terrace. He peers down the garden and heads for the exit

The security lights come on in the garden

Jim Grant appears out of the shadows

George Jesus!
Jim I hope I didn't startle you.
George No, that's all right.
Jim I saw the lights going on and off and came through the garden. I was concerned. I didn't know Nell had a visitor ...
George A visitor? Well, I wouldn't say a visitor exactly ...
Jim (*studying George*) More of a friend?
George A friend? No — more of a relative.
Jim A relative?
George My wife and Nell are like sisters. Known each other for years ...
Jim I see.
George I do a few odd jobs around here. (*He glances up at the house*) Those barge boards need fixing. And how's this swing seat doing? (*He swings the seat back and forward*) Had to reassemble it the other day.
Jim Did you?
George Yes, that's much better. It was making a terrible noise. (*He sits on the seat and swings*) Seems all right now.
Jim You're George Rush, aren't you?
George What?
Jim You're George Rush.
George Yes, much smoother.
Jim My name's Jim Grant. I live in the village.
George Do you? Why don't you go inside, Jim? I'm just off.
Jim Do you have far to go?
George Far? Depends on what you call far.
Jim You don't live in the village?
George No, I certainly don't live in the village.
Jim Then where do you live?
George (*with a vague gesture*) Over there.
Jim Over there?
George Yes.
Jim You mean Brimley?
George (*glancing upwards*) Those spoutings will have to be repainted. That's another job.
Jim You know you surprise me. I didn't realize poets could be so practical.
George I surprise myself sometimes.
Jim Did you sign my book?
George Yes, under the dedication to my dear wife. I left it on the sideboard. If you want to get it I'm just ... (*He half-rises*)
Jim Before you go... (*He joins George on the seat*)

They swing the seat as they talk

I suppose you've known Nell a long time.
George Well, my wife has.
Jim I find her very attractive.
George (*completely surprised*) Do you? Nell? Oh.
Jim Don't you?
George I hadn't really thought about it. (*He muses*) Old Nell... Hm.
(*Doubtfully*) I suppose you could call her attractive.
Jim I just wondered if you thought I stood a chance?
George (*regarding Jim incredulously*) What — you and old Nell?
Jim She's not old.
George No, not that old, I suppose.
Jim Well, what do you think?
George What?
Jim Do I stand a chance?
George I don't see why not. After all, she is on her own, poor soul.
Jim Yes, but I can't believe there isn't someone else.
George Someone else?

They swing the seat faster

Jim She's a little evasive on the subject. But I can't help feeling there must
be someone — somewhere ...
George She has a temper of course.
Jim Does she?
George Terrible.
Jim I did ask her if there was someone ...
George What did she say?
Jim She said there was someone once ... It had been quite passionate for a
time but recently it had begun to wane ...

They stop swinging

*During the following, Nell appears at the terrace door, now wearing a shirt
and slacks. She leans by the door, arms folded, listening*

George (*staring*) Wane? (*Thoughtfully*) Wane ... Now who could it be?
Jim Perhaps someone from the office?
George Yes ...
Jim But then, she's only been there a short time.
George But how did she get the job? I mean she's totally inexperienced and
she can't spell. Perhaps it was someone she knew before, doing her a favour
— know what I mean?

Jim Apparently he's married with children.

George There's someone married with children at the office. I remember her talking about him. This begins to add up.

Jim Still, it's on the wane.

George Yes, but a word of caution, Jim. Don't rush things. Step by step. Remember she's had a bad experience — it's made her bitter. You have to see her in all her moods.

Jim Moods?

George She has moods, Jim. She comes with a lot of emotional baggage … (*He becomes aware of Nell's presence and his voice dies away*)

Nell Don't let me keep you, George. I know Helen must be getting worried.

George Right.

Nell (*mischievously*) And I know Jim wants to show me his hose attachment …

George (*standing*) Yes. Well. (*He pushes the swing seat*) I don't think you'll have any more trouble with that.

Nell What?

George The seat.

Nell Oh. Yes.

George heads slowly for the garden exit L, running a professional hand over the drainpipe as he does so

    George exits

Nell Come in, Jim — it's getting cold out here.

Nell and Jim move into the drawing-room

Nell You seemed to be talking very intently.

Jim We were talking about you.

Nell My favourite subject. Let me get you a drink. (*She pours Jim a drink*)

Jim straightens a picture with great deliberation

    Do you like that picture, Jim?

Jim It wasn't straight.

Nell But do you like it?

Jim What is it supposed to be?

Nell Rain and mist over Exmoor.

Jim Can't see much.

Nell Well, you wouldn't, would you?

Jim Pity he didn't pick a better day.

Nell (*smiling*) I think that's the point, Jim. (*She hands him his drink*) What did he say about me?

Jim Who?

Nell George Rush.

Jim I asked him if there was anyone else. I thought he'd know. I hope you don't mind.

Nell No. (*Pause*) And was there?

Jim He seemed to find the idea amusing.

Nell Did he?

Jim He seemed to think you had too much emotional baggage — that you were too bitter to form a lasting relationship.

Nell He said that, did he?

Jim Yes. He advised caution.

Nell That sounds like him.

Jim He thought there might be someone at the office.

Nell Did he?

Jim I didn't believe him. I believe it's someone closer to home …

Nell Jim, you're prying again.

Jim I'm sorry. I just wondered if we had a future, that was all.

Nell Jim, this is the future. We've cashed our Peps, both of us. We had a past, present and a future once — not any more. This is it.

Jim I'll drink to that, Nell. My future went out with the tide at Ramsgate.

Nell Mine went out the door with three suitcases and a set of golf clubs.

Jim So it's live for the moment, Nell. And don't give a damn.

Nell Yes.

Jim (*putting his drink down*) Do you mind if I kiss you?

Nell (*smiling*) Do you normally ask, Jim?

Jim Yes.

Nell We don't on this side of the village …

Jim kisses Nell. They move into an embrace

CURTAIN

ACT II

SCENE 1

The same. Two weeks later. Noon

The hot weather continues

A man's shirt lies discarded on the swing seat. A hoe leans against an outside wall of the house. There is a box of chocolates in the shade of the canopy

The CURTAIN *rises. Nell enters from the house. She is wearing shorts and a suntop and is carrying a jug of lemonade and some glasses on a tray*

There is the sound of a car approaching

Nell frowns. She sets down the drinks in front of the swing seat and moves to investigate

Gail enters through the garden L. *She looks a little breathless*

Gail I've got Helen with me.

Nell What!

Gail I couldn't help it. I met her in Boots and I happened to mention I was popping over, and she insisted on coming. So if there's any incriminating evidence, anything tying you in with George, get rid of it, wherever it is.

Nell Why?

Gail Because she wants to look round.

Nell Why should she want to look round? Where is she?

Gail In the car. She wanted me to mention it to you first.

Nell Mention what?

Gail You're not going to like this, Nell. She wants to buy the house.

Nell (*after a pause*) You're right. I don't like it.

Gail Does it matter?

Nell Of course it matters. I know her. I'd hate the thought of her living here. Besides, they couldn't afford it. George hasn't got any money.

Gail No, but his father has — and he's failing fast. Any day now, Nell.

Nell George never said his father had money.

Gail He had fish and chip shops, so they probably wanted to keep quiet about it. Apparently he's got plenty.

Nell My God.

Gail And George was the only child so they could easily afford it. You'll probably get top price, Nell.

Nell I don't know if I want to sell. Not now I've got a job.

Gail (*after a hesitation*) That may not be so permanent. I'd go for a quick sale.

Nell What do you mean?

Gail Terry's not very pleased with you.

Nell How do you know?

Gail I know.

Nell Has he been talking about me?

Gail He doesn't like your sarcasm, Nell.

Nell What sarcasm?

Gail Well, you know how he's neglected himself since his wife left him — hardly bothering to shave, never presses his suits, never irons his shirts …

Nell I know that.

Gail Well, when he comes in like that it's not advisable to say, "Going somewhere special today, Mr Pearson?" He's not insensitive. And he has had a rough time.

Nell We've all had a rough time, Gail. We don't all fall apart. I've no patience with him.

Gail It's not a question of whether you have patience with him — it's whether he has patience with you.

Nell As bad as that?

Gail Apart from the sarcasm, there's the word processor — they still haven't got to the bottom of that. And then there's the photocopier. I did point out nevertheless that you were very good with people.

Nell What did he say?

Gail He said having seen you with machines he shuddered to think what you were like with people. I told him all you needed was a little self-confidence.

Nell You're right. If I lose that job has he any idea what that would do to my self-confidence?

Gail I told him that. He said that he'd only known you a short time but he didn't think self-confidence was one of your problems.

Nell Oh. Well, don't worry about me. I'll survive, Gail. (*She glances down the garden*) I just wish you hadn't brought her this morning.

Gail What? (*She follows Nell's glance and spots the shirt on the swing seat*) Oh, my God! He's here, isn't he?

Nell is about to reply but ——

Helen enters the garden from L

Gail sits down on the shirt and tries to look casual

Nell Hallo, Helen.

Helen Has Gail told you why I'm here?

Nell Yes.

Helen You don't mind?

Nell Not at all. I'm just not sure I want to sell.

Helen Do you have any choice, Nell? You're being very brave, I know. But with all those debts money must be a problem.

Nell (*lightly*) Oh, I don't know, I could always sell the Renoir.

Helen You haven't got a Renoir.

Nell It was a joke, Helen.

Helen Is it because you know me? Would you sooner sell to a stranger? I would understand. It's not so much for myself — it's for George.

Nell George?

Helen He's always loved this house.

Helen sits by Gail, who tucks the shirt further out of sight

And now his father's fading …

Nell His father. Is that the one who lives in your garage?

Helen (*frowning*) It's not a garage. It's a conversion — a self-contained flat.

Nell Of course. I don't know why I keep thinking of it as a garage — probably because it still looks like a garage.

Gail (*hastily*) Why doesn't Helen look around the house now, Nell? I haven't much time.

Helen I would like to look at the main bedroom.

Nell Bedroom. Why?

Helen I'm a little concerned about the dimensions. George loves a big bedroom.

Nell I think he'll find it big enough — unless he's contemplating double somersaults.

Gail Why don't you go and measure it, Helen? That would be best.

Helen makes to rise but stops

Helen Who's that coming up the garden?

Gail groans silently

Jim comes into view. He is wearing a vest and slacks

Gail's expression changes; her mouth drops open. Helen regards Jim curiously

Nell Gail. Helen. This is Jim. He lives in the village.

They all greet each other

Jim (*after a hesitation*) I think you're sitting on my shirt.
Gail Oh, sorry.

Gail hands Jim the very crumpled and wrinkled shirt. He stares at it and slips it on

Jim It was hot down there.
Nell Sit down, Jim. I'll pour you some lemonade.

Jim sits with Helen and Gail as Nell busies herself pouring Jim a drink

Helen They say it's hotter than Madrid.
Jim Yes, I've heard that.
Gail They're talking about water rationing.
Jim I've stopped using my hosepipe.
Helen So have we.
Jim (*after a pause*) My brother-in-law slept with his head in the fridge last night.
Helen Good heavens.
Gail How did he manage that?
Jim Took all the trays out — everything — then put cushions in — and then his head.
Helen The things people do.
Jim It's worse at night.
Gail They say a man tried to sleep on his roof in Brimley and fell off.
Jim Yes, I heard that.

George enters R *behind of the swing seat*

Unaware that the seat is occupied, George sees Nell standing on the terrace, supposedly alone. He picks up the hoe that's leaning against the wall and approaches Nell

During the following the occupants of the swing seat stare at each other in astonishment. Nell regards George in icy silence

George (*in a Mummerset accent*) Lovely weather, missis. Mind, we need the rain. Nothing's germinating. Blight all over the country. Sheep look none too healthy — putting on no weight at all … We'll get no hay this year, mark my words. And that'll make fodder a price come Michaelmas. (*He leers at Nell*) Now, missis, would you like me to turn your bed over or attend to your seedlings?

Helen stands, followed by the others. They stare over the canopy. George gapes. Nell enjoys George's discomfort

Helen (*surprised*) George, what are you doing here?
George What?
Helen I thought you were conducting cycling proficiency tests?
George Finished early.
Helen How did you know I was here?
George What?
Helen Stop behaving as if you're half-witted, George. Why have you come?
George (*after a hesitation*)Well, why have you come?
Helen To look at the house.
George Damn. And I was going to surprise you.
Helen You too? Isn't that incredible, Nell?
Nell Very.
Helen Two minds but a single thought. It's always happening. I suppose it's being married for so long.
Nell Well, now you're here, George, you and Helen can look round together — you can measure the bedroom …
George What?
Helen Come along, George.

Helen takes George by the hand and leads him into the house. Jim exchanges a glance with Nell and raises his eyebrows. Gail regards Jim and Nell with interest

Nell (*acidly*) Would you go round with them, Gail — I'm concerned for the silver.

Gail looks from one to the other

Gail Yes. Right.

Gail gives Jim and Nell a conspiratorial smile and exits into the house

Jim It's George Rush, isn't it?
Nell What makes you think that?
Jim It's fairly obvious. Besides, he's the type.
Nell What do you mean — the type?
Jim I wasn't sure if I should mention this but I was at a dinner a few days ago and his name cropped up …
Nell (*drily*) I wonder why?
Jim All right, I mentioned him. I was curious. There were a couple of teachers at the table and I mentioned this teacher who had written some

verse. One of them knew — a Mrs Williams. She was on a visit. She lives in Ipswich. Perhaps you remember her.

Nell Mrs Williams?

Jim She taught physical education to the girls.

Nell Oh yes. I remember. Quite attractive. Didn't stay long.

Jim Long enough.

Nell What do you mean?

Jim She seemed to remember George Rush rather well. In fact, when I mentioned his name I thought she turned pale.

Nell He often has that effect.

Jim I didn't pursue it at the time but later, several drinks later, when we were alone, she told me everything.

Nell Everything?

Jim He seduced her at a party.

Nell (*incredulously*) Mrs Williams?

Jim Yes.

Nell He couldn't have done. What do you mean — seduced? What party? George hates parties.

Jim It was at their house — about four years ago. End of term. Some teachers — a few parents.

Nell Wait a minute. I was at that party. We were almost the last to leave. It couldn't have happened there.

Jim (*distastefully*) It took place in the bathroom.

Nell (*staring*) The bathroom?

Jim It was a brief encounter.

Nell It must have been. I don't believe her.

Jim She must have thought I didn't either. When she returned to Ipswich she sent me a letter he wrote to her.

Nell Wrote to her? George never puts anything in writing.

Jim takes a piece of notepaper from his pocket and hands it to Nell

Jim It's just the final page. You may recognize the writing. You'll certainly recognize the verse. You'll see it's signed "G".

Nell studies the note

Nell You've been very thorough. Why did she send this to you?

Jim I told her a friend of mine had become entangled with George Rush.

Nell You discussed me with Mrs Williams

Jim Not by name. (*Pause*) Would you like to keep it?

Nell Are you sure you don't want to run off a few copies?

Jim That's not fair, Nell. I was only thinking of you.

Nell You were thinking of yourself, Jim. And in future, don't spy on my
friends, and don't talk about them behind their backs.

Jim Oh. (*Stiffly*) Perhaps I'd better go.

Nell Yes.

Jim I'll walk back through the garden. (*He holds his hand out for the letter*)

Nell continues to study the letter

Jim smiles faintly and exits L *through the garden*

Gail enters from the house

Gail They're doing their arithmetic. I thought I'd leave them to it. (*She looks
around*) Oh, has he gone?

Nell Yes.

Gail He looked nice. (*Pause*) What was he doing here?

Nell Cutting the hedge.

Gail Is he married?

Nell Widowed.

Gail And he's cutting your hedge … Play your cards right, Nell and it could
lead to something else …

Nell It has — he's going to do the lawns as well.

Gail You know what I mean.

Gail spots the box of chocolates in the shade of the canopy

Gail Chocolates. Did he bring those as well?

Nell Well, it wasn't George. He never brings anything.

Gail He's certainly a better bet than George.

Nell Don't start matchmaking, Gail.

Gail Nell, you need someone permanent in your life — someone to look after
you. Living out here all alone — don't you ever get frightened at nights?

Nell No, I keep John's old shotgun under the bed.

Gail A gun under the bed! You won't get a man that way.

Nell It's to keep them out of the bed — not get them into it.

The sound of Helen's and George's voices comes from the house

Nell Look, get rid of them, will you? I want to be on my own for a while.

Gail sighs, shrugs and exits through the drawing-room

Nell continues studying the letter

We hear the sounds of the front door slamming and a car starting and driving away

Nell puts the note down on the low table. She pours some lemonade

George enters the terrace from L. *He regards Nell diffidently*

Nell I thought you'd gone.

George She left me to make an offer. Don't worry, I'm not going to. I couldn't live here — too many memories.

Nell Is that why you stayed away? It's been two weeks, George. Two weeks without a word and I was almost suicidal that night.

George I knew you were all right, Nell.

Nell How? Did you ring the morgue?

George It's been difficult. Dad's failing, I'm afraid. But we've got plenty of time now. We're supposed to be haggling. (*He sits close to Nell*) Do you know I have the strong desire to see you in black underwear ...

Nell I'll stop washing it.

George (*seeing the chocolate box*) Chocolates. (*He helps himself to a chocolate*) Who brought these?

Nell Jim.

George Oh. Has he been around much?

Nell Yes. Do you mind?

George No. I'm glad you weren't on your own. You should see more people.

Nell spreads the letter carefully out on the table

Nell Would you like some lemonade?

George Thanks.

Nell I'll get you a clean glass ...

Nell goes into the drawing-room, takes a glass from the sideboard and watches George from the window during the following

George helps himself to another chocolate. He notices the letter and looks at it curiously. He moves in to get a closer look. He is about to return to the chocolates when he stops, thunderstruck. He snatches up the letter in a panic

Nell comes out of the house with the glass

Nell I see you're reading the letter.

George (*wildly*) Letter?

Nell The one you're holding.

George Where did it come from?
Nell Don't you know?
George (*weakly*) Writing looks familiar...
Nell It should do — it's yours. It's just the last page. You'll see it's signed "G". That's typical of you, isn't it? Having finally decided to put pen to paper and declare yourself — the sudden sense of caution. 'Yours, "G"'. It could have been almost anyone. Well, anyone with the initial "G", that is. But of course I recognized the verse.
George But where did it come from?
Nell Mrs Williams.
George Williams?
Nell Mrs Maxine Williams. Never trust a woman with a name like Maxine, George. And you did trust her, didn't you? You've never written me a letter. Perhaps I should move to Ipswich.
George Ipswich?
Nell Careful, George. You're beginning to sound half-witted again. You remember Mrs Williams — the life and soul of the gym, expert on the parallel bars and all things horizontal...
George But why did she send this to you?
Nell She was concerned about me. She feels that no woman should go through what she went through. She still daren't enter a bathroom unaccompanied.
George Bathroom?
Nell Yes, bathroom. Now do you remember? Is she another golden thread, George? Weren't you supposed to be pining for me in those days? It confirms what I've always thought about you. You'd leap on anything with a pulse.
George It wasn't like that, Nell. It was the end of term. We were both physically and mentally exhausted ——
Nell Not physically, George.
George And you were unapproachable.
Nell I think I'm going to get the blame for this.
George I found her crying in the bathroom.
Nell What were you doing in there — hiding in the shower?
George It was a mad impulse.
Nell You've never acted on impulse in your life. Why did you write that letter? Did you expect to be in Ipswich for the weekend?
George No, I wrote because I didn't want her to feel degraded by the incident.
Nell Degraded! I'm the one who feels degraded — write me a letter.
George It's all in the past, Nell. I'd almost forgotten.
Nell Mrs Williams hasn't forgotten. She still bears the marks of the bathroom scales.

George I still don't understand why she sent you the letter — after all this time. How did she know about us? How did she find your address? I don't understand ... (*He selects another chocolate but stops before eating it*) Oh, yes, I do. It was Jim, wasn't it? The wedge. Still trying to come between us. How did he know about Mrs Williams?

Nell remains silent

It doesn't matter. He'll have ways of finding things out. And he's the sort who'd read other people's letters. I think you'll agree that's a pretty low thing to do.
Nell Yes, but on the scale of wrongdoing it falls a little below infidelity.
George So it was him. Well, don't let him fool you. Can't you see what he's doing? He's trying to wheedle himself in here. He may seem harmless but don't trust him, Nell. (*Pause*) No matter how harmless he seems ...

Nell is silent

He is harmless — isn't he?

Nell doesn't reply

George My God! You mean it's happened?
Nell I'm sorry, George. (*She turns away*)
George Poor Nell.
Nell (*turning and staring at him in astonishment*) You don't mind?
George Of course I mind. But how can I reproach you? It would be hypocritical.
Nell That's true.

George takes another chocolate and chews it thoughtfully

George Poor Nell. Was it that night — the night he came here? The night I left you alone with him?
Nell Yes.
George Poor Nell.
Nell Don't keep saying that! (*Pause*) If it's any consolation, I felt ashamed of myself.
George You've nothing to be ashamed of.
Nell I thought I had. The guilt was terrible — I spent hours in the shower trying to wash it away.
George (*chewing mournfully*) It won't wash away, Nell. I know, I've tried.
Nell You're not jealous? Only I notice you're still eating his chocolates.

George Of course I'm jealous but I've no right to be. I'm sorry, Nell.

Nell Will you stop looking at me as if I'm an invalid... (*She goes into the drawing-room*)

George (*picking up the chocolates and following Nell*) Where did it happen, Nell?

Nell (*staring*) What?

George I just don't like to think it happened in our room.

Nell Our room! Do you mean my room?

George (*looking around the drawing-room*) Did it happen here?

Nell What are you looking for? An outline in chalk?

George All right. Don't tell me. I don't want to know. (*Pause*) What happened afterwards?

Nell Afterwards?

George Yes.

Nell We released a flock of pigeons and fired a rocket. What do you think happened?

George I mean, did he stay the night?

Nell No.

George That's something, I suppose.

Nell What do you mean, that's something? You don't stay the night.

George I mean, we're not going to let one mistake spoil things. We have something special, Nell. We're not throwing that away because of one mistake ...

Nell is silent again. George studies her. Nell begins to straighten the room

It was one mistake ... ?

Nell No, it happened again.

George Twice!

Nell It has been two weeks, George. Two weeks without a word.

George (*angrily*) It's a good thing it wasn't a month — you'd have probably become engaged. Twice!

Nell Does it make any difference?

George Of course it makes a difference. Where did twice happen?

Nell Not where again.

George Yes — where?

Nell I didn't plan it. He'd been ringing me five, six times a day. We went out for dinner. I didn't expect it to happen.

George Where?

Nell At his house. He asked me back for a coffee.

George You went back to his house! After all that had happened?

Nell It seemed impolite to refuse.

George And that's not the only thing it seemed impolite to refuse. He couldn't have taken you by surprise — not at his age. Did you take another shower afterwards to remove the guilt — or do you find it takes less soap and water these days?

Nell turns away

Don't turn away. You don't know how I feel. What this is doing to me.
Nell (*turning back*) Oh, we're back to you again, are we?
George I feel empty inside.
Nell (*holding the chocolates out to George*) Have a chocolate.

George knocks the box to the ground

Temper, George.
George And what was it like the second time? Did you respond? Did you sigh? Did you have time to remove your earrings and squirt a little perfume? Or was he on you before you could say Viagra? When I think how you've reproached me and all the time this was going on ——
Nell It wasn't ——
George — behind my back.
Nell It wasn't behind your back.
George The times you sat here looking at me with that expression — like Queen Victoria in mourning for Albert. And all the time you were waiting for some rich widower to come along to this gilded fly trap.
Nell (*angrily*) Gilded what?
George Fly trap! And now you'll be able to keep it. Keep your precious house that means so much more to you than me.
Nell George, I'd have lived with you in a shed.
George That's easy to say, isn't it? I can just see you two settling down here. All your problems solved.
Nell Actually, he plans a world cruise next year. He's asked me to go with him.
George Has he? You've fallen on your feet, Nell. He wants you to share his declining years.
Nell He's not declining.
George Well, you can certainly vouch for that. And his wife barely cold.
Nell She was cremated.
George An accountant — and dull as ditchwater.
Nell At least he doesn't think he's Dylan Thomas after half a bottle of wine.
George That's what surprises me. That you can see anything in someone so utterly boring.
Nell You don't know him.

George I've met him. Jim Grant, the life and soul of any funeral. I bet his wife wasn't washed off that sea front — I bet she jumped.

Nell That's a terrible thing to say.

George And while his wife's ashes are blowing in the wind you'll both be on the deck of the QE2. Jim in his white tuxedo, the sun glinting on his dentures ——

Nell He has his own teeth ——

George — and you clutching his arm, dressed in an expensive gown, and gazing towards Hawaii. Both of you looking like an advert for a Saga holiday.

Nell I must say you make it sound quite attractive. Preferable to Withernsea, or Yarmouth or wherever you and Helen and Muffin, Puffin and Pompom go every year — not forgetting Buttons the dog.

George (*glaring at Nell*) My God! I've read about lips curling in disdain but yours actually do. Well, you may have got away with that haughty expression twenty years ago but now it looks faintly ridiculous.

Nell Does it really?

George Ah. Now I see the attraction. That's it, isn't it? He makes you look younger. You only have to stand next to that old coffin-dodger and the years just fall away. Let's face it — he'd make any one look young.

Nell kicks George hard on the shin. He staggers back in pain and surprise

George (*after a pause*) Are you trying to get rid of me?

Nell Yes.

George That hurt.

Nell It was meant to.

George I see. You're both waiting for me to go, aren't you? What a fool I've been. He's sitting out there in the car, isn't he? Clutching his mobile …

The phone rings. George snatches it up

George (*into the phone; snarling*) Get out of our lives, you bastard. (*He stops*) What? … Oh. (*He holds the phone out to Nell*) It's someone called Terry from the office.

Nell glares at George and takes the phone

George exits with a dignified limp

CURTAIN

SCENE 2

The same. Mid-evening. A week later

The Lights are on in the drawing-room. The terrace is in darkness

When the CURTAIN *rises, George is sitting in an armchair wearing a battered raincoat and looking a little worse for wear*

Nell enters from the hall wearing an evening dress and carrying her earrings. She crosses to the window, slipping the earrings on

George rises unsteadily from an armchair

Nell (*starting back*) Oh God! It's you.

George (*in a nasal tone*) Excuse me, madam. I'm here on behalf of Dreamland Mattresses. I understand from head office that there's been a complaint regarding your springing. The Venus model, I believe, which is normally able to withstand most wear and tear …

Nell checks the contents of her handbag during the following

But for excessive or prolonged use we recommend the Dreadnought. (*Pause*) Has there been excessive or prolonged use, madam?

Nell (*coldly*) No.

George Would you care for me to test the said springing?

Nell Are you qualified?

George I am our chief test pilot, madam. I am prepared to give a demonstration even as we speak. (*Pause*) If required.

Nell It isn't required.

George Pity. (*He slumps back in his chair*)

Nell I think you'd better give me your key back, George.

George "Give me your key back, George". My, we've certainly changed since old moneybags has come on the scene.

Nell Have you been drinking?

George I may have fallen off a couple of bar stools.

Nell Is this the behaviour of a man who conducts the cycling proficiency tests? Suppose you'd had an accident?

George You wouldn't have cared.

Nell Stop feeling sorry for yourself. (*She looks anxiously out of the window* US)

George Are you going out?

Nell No, I'm knitting a sweater. Of course I'm going out.

George I'll come with you.

Nell You can't. It's the Midsummer Ball. It's formal.

George Then you're certainly going with the right man. He's as formal as a tax demand — and about as pleasant. And where's this ball talking place? I may wish to attend. I merely have to ring my tailor …

Nell It's at the castle.

George Oh. Does Jim know the Duke? Is he in residence?

Nell I believe so.

George My word, socially your feet don't touch the ground these days, do they, Nell?

Nell George, if I'd waited for you to take me out I'd have waited forever.

George And when's rat face coming?

Nell Any minute — and don't call him that.

George Sorry. This Midsummer Ball, is it for charity?

Nell Yes.

George Is it for people with — rickets? Is it for orphans?

Nell Heart Foundation.

George Oh. Is he hoping to get one?

Nell It's a good cause and he's done a great deal of work.

George (*scornfully*) That's conscience. Take the bread from people's mouths Monday to Friday — and give them a few crumbs back at the weekend.

Nell I do believe you're turning into a socialist, George.

George I've been finding a few things out about our Mr Gradgrind. (*Solemnly*) Did you know he sacked his oldest clerk at a minute's notice — an old man who'd been with him over thirty years. (*Confidentially*) This old clerk said he was an absolute bastard.

Nell Well, he would, wouldn't he? And where did you meet this old clerk?

George In a pub. I met the poor old bugger in a pub. He was bent almost double.

Nell Why was he bent almost double, George?

George Arthritis. Do you know when that bastard made him take his extra week's holiday? March.

Nell Well, at least he'd be able to get a deckchair.

George And what about the bloody perfect marriage?

Nell Did the old clerk tell you about that too?

George Yes. And it wasn't so bloody perfect. She was terrified of him. Terrified of him. She scraped his car once — practically hid in the cupboard for a fortnight.

Nell And how did the old clerk know that?

George He knew. He knew. He knew the cleaning lady. Bloody terrified of him.

Nell Stop swearing, George.

George An absolute bastard. A martinet. Every morning, egg had to be lightly poached, bacon well-grilled, toast crisp — otherwise, back in her face. New dresses — under the bed. Shoes — confiscated. Death must have been a welcome relief. I bet she jumped.

Nell George, I'm in a hurry. And Jim won't come while you're here.

George How does he know I'm here? Does he have the house under a telescope?

Nell I'd better ring him on his carphone. (*She moves to the phone*)

George follows Nell

George Oh, yes, the carphone. And does he have a filofax in there as well? And a lap top computer — and floppy disks? And is he on the internet?

Nell Yes, he is, as a matter of fact.

George My word, he's as modern as tomorrow.

Nell George, we haven't time for this.

George Have you been in his garage yet? Does he have a jar for screws labelled: "Screws — three eighths"? Does he have a jar for nails labelled, "Nails — two inches"?

Nell (*warningly*) George.

George Does he have a sweater with little golfers on it?

Nell I've no idea but he certainly doesn't have fluffy lavatory seat covers.

George That's right, throw those lavatory seat covers back in my face.

Nell What did you come for, George?

George (*straightening himself up with great dignity*) Before you make that phone call, I'd like to collect a few of my personal possessions left here in happier times: my spare razor, my personal soap — if he hasn't used it — and that picture of me taken in Bruges.

Nell I was in that picture too.

George Then cut me out. Don't want any inferences drawn — particularly since it's kept in the bedroom — and since I won't be coming here any more.

Nell Inferences! There were twenty-five boys in that picture — apart from us.

George Nevertheless, your hand is resting on my shoulder and the picture is on your bedside table. I just hope those twenty-five boys haven't been looking down on scenes that might deprave and corrupt them.

Nell Don't worry — they haven't.

There is the sound of a car approaching and stopping

I'll get your things.

Nell exits into the hall

George makes himself comfortable

Jim enters from the hall. He is wearing an evening-suit. He eyes George coldly

George Oh, you're using the front door now, are you, Jimbo?
Jim I thought it was you.
George Did you?
Jim I recognized the car.
George Ah, do you have the number in your filofax?
Jim I recognized it because of the state it was in. Your exhaust's falling off and you have a bald spot on your rear tyre.
George Damn! I usually try to park it so the bald spot's on the ground.
Jim It wouldn't pass its MOT. And there are other road users to consider.
George You're right. I'll change it. (*With great politeness*) Do you have a wheel brace and jack to hand? And possibly one of those reflective triangles. I'm sure you do. It does mean I shall be here for some time.
Jim No, you won't.
George Pardon?
Jim Don't underestimate me, George. People have been doing that all my life.
George Have they ever been wrong?
Jim I've got nothing against you personally but you're in the way.
George And what happens to people that get in your way, Jim?
Jim I haven't time for this.
George You wouldn't like her, Jim. She has a terrible temper. The first six weeks are all right but after that — watch out. And the moods …
Jim That may have something to do with you. People can change.
George And are you going to change her, Jim?
Jim Possibly. But that needn't concern you. I want you to leave.
George I'm not leaving.
Jim Then I'll have to make you.
George And how do you intend to do that?
Jim By any means necessary.
George I'm not leaving. (*He settles back in the chair*) I'm a key holder.
Jim I'd like the key as well.
George No.
Jim George, if you don't give me the key and leave I'll pick up that phone and ring your wife.
George (*staring*) What?
Jim Helen, isn't it? I know the number. (*He smiles*) I have it in my filofax. I'll ask her to fetch you. I'll tell her you've been drinking, that you're making a nuisance of yourself — and why. That should do it.
George (*shocked*) You wouldn't.

Jim Try me, George.
George (*rising unsteadily*) I need some fresh air. (*He moves towards the terrace*)
Jim The key, George.

George hesitates and then throws the key down on the carpet

George The old clerk was right — an absolute bastard ...

George exits into garden and disappears into the darkness

Jim smiles and picks up the key

Nell enters from the hall. She is carrying George's things in a carrier bag

Nell Where's George?
Jim He's gone.
Nell He'll be back.
Jim No. I have his key.
Nell (*staring*) He gave it to you?
Jim Yes.
Nell I never thought he would.
Jim So we can lock up. You shouldn't have any more trouble.
Nell Don't you believe it. He'll probably come in through the cat flap.
Jim Nell, we're late. We were late to start with and it's getting later. You know this evening's important to me.
Nell I'm sorry, Jim. But he's been drinking.
Jim He can sleep it off in the car.
Nell (*looking out on to the terrace*) I remember when this house meant peace and tranquillity. Now it's like King's Cross station — it even has dossers. I shall be glad to leave.
Jim That's not true, is it, Nell? You love this place — that's why you keep putting off the sale. You're only selling because of the sixty-five thousand pounds.
Nell (*staring*) How did you know the amount? I've never told anyone.
Jim (*smiling*) I have ways...
Nell That's what George said.
Jim Sixty-five thousand, seven hundred and fifty-six, to be precise.
Nell (*coldly*) You sound like my bank manager. He always knows the exact amount. I think he has it written on his cuff. I thought these things were confidential.
Jim They are of course but ——
Nell But there are ways. I don't like this, Jim. I don't like this prying.

Jim You don't understand. I want to help you. I'm the only one who can. I can pay it off.

Nell What?

Jim Then you'll have no need to sell.

Nell (*shocked*) Sixty-five thousand?

Jim Yes.

Nell And what do you want in return, Jim?

Jim Nothing. No strings. What makes you happy, makes me happy. And it's something I can do ... After all, Nell, it's still a man's world ... Will you let me?

Nell Oh, Jim, to wake up just once and not feel the great weight of that debt bearing down on me ...

Nell kisses Jim. He embraces her

George enters unexpectedly from the hall

Nell and Jim move apart

George (*touching his forelock*) Excuse me, madam. British Gas. I'm investigating an unconfirmed report of an excessive build-up of inflammable vapours. It could be hot air but I must advise you not to light up in here or cause any unnecessary friction.

Jim (*impatiently*) We haven't time for this nonsense.

George Excuse my casual attire, madam, but I was on my way to a poetry reading when I was called out. Now, I shall have to check your dials and I'll require a sprocket wrench. Do you have one to hand?

Nell (*with a sad smile*) No.

George What a pity. (*He turns to Jim*) Do you have a sprocket wrench in your car, sir — along with your wheel brace and matching ring spanners?

Jim For God's sake!

Nell There's just one small point — we don't have gas.

George Ah. (*He glances at Jim*) Then it must be hot air.

Jim Nell, we haven't time to play these games.

Jim glances at his watch

George Oh, dear. Jim's looking at his watch.

Nell I'm sorry, Jim.

George Did you hear that. She's sorry. She's never said that to me. And in such a warm tone. Don't be impatient, Jimbo — if a thing's worth having, it's worth waiting for.

Nell Now he's a philosopher.

George Notice the change in tone, Jimbo.
Jim Don't call me that. Why don't you go and sit in your car?
George Oh, dear. Jimbo's annoyed with me. What are you going to do,
Jimbo — make that call?

Jim is silent

Nell What call? What does he mean?
Jim I don't know what he means. He's drunk.
George Not that drunk. He threatened to ring Helen — tell her everything.
Nell Did you, Jim?

Jim remains silent

George Nothing to say? Jim "don't underrate me" Grant? What are you
going to tell her? That you didn't mean it? That it was an empty threat?
Jim I don't make empty threats.
George Then ring her, Jim.
Jim I don't have the number with me …
George Then I'll make it easy for you. I'll dial it. (*He picks up the phone,
dials the number and listens*) It's ringing.

George hands the phone to Jim. Jim puts the phone to his ear

Jim (*into the phone*) Hallo.
Nell No!

*Nell snatches the phone from Jim and replaces it. Jim looks at her in surprise.
George sits down, exhausted*

Jim I'm going to my car now. I expect you to come at once. I shan't wait.
(*He glances at George*) God! What did you ever see in this weasel?

Jim exits

George (*standing*) Weasel! Did you hear that? Did I act like a weasel, Nell?
Nell No, George — for the first time I was proud of you.
George But you stopped him.
Nell Yes.
George Why?
Nell I remembered how I felt when I got that letter from John. Until then I
was so sure of myself — just like Helen. I was sure of my clothes, my sense
of humour, my looks, everything. And he took it all away. That's what I

can't forgive him for — he made me feel ugly. (*Pause*) He called the other day.

George (*surprised*) John did?

Nell Yes. He came to discuss Christopher's future. He looked older — I suppose he thought I did. When he left he kissed me hard on the mouth and said, "It's a long time since I had a kiss like that".

George What did you say?

Nell Nothing. I felt nothing. It was too late.

There is the sound of a car departing

George He's gone.

Nell Now what am I going to do? All dressed up and no place to go.

George Should we go up?

Nell I'd sooner roll naked in a bed of nettles.

George I can stay the night, Nell.

Nell What?

George My bag's in the car.

Nell And where are you tonight, George?

George Student Drama Festival. Harrogate.

Nell You never change. Don't you realize we're finished. Mrs Williams was the end, George.

George The end?

Nell You know, when you see the big movie and those letters come up saying "The End", and everyone leaves the cinema. Well, this is it — "The End".

George No, we always ride off into the sunset, Nell. There's too much between us. Too much laughter, too many tears. What we've got is something special — once in a lifetime, Nell.

George holds Nell

Nell (*quietly*) You think you can tiptoe through my life without leaving a footprint, don't you, George?

George I've always been light on my feet. (*Pause*) Well, should we go up?

Nell Why? To lock limbs, crash into the quilt, enter the gates of ecstasy?

George No, to make love. Because I love you, Nell. I never realized how much until now.

George kisses Nell. She leans back and studies him for a moment

Nell I think I'd better get out of the silks and satins.

George I'll put the car down the lane.

Nell shakes her head and sighs. The phone rings

Nell That'll be Jim. Leave it.

Nell exits

George hesitates. He closes the hall door and picks up the phone

George (*into the phone*) Hallo. This is the Easy-Squeezy Corset Company here. Can we supply you with a long-felt want?

The caller rings off. George smiles. He replaces the phone, hesitates and then disconnects it. He punches the air in victory

George exits

CURTAIN

SCENE 3

The same. The next day

It is mid-morning. The sun is bright on the terrace

The CURTAIN *rises. Nell enters from the house. She is wearing a bathrobe and carrying a tray with a coffee pot and two cups on it. She places the tray on the low table, sits on the swing seat and puts on her sunglasses*

Helen enters the terrace from L

Nell (*removing her glasses in surprise*) Helen! (*She gives an anxious glance towards the drawing-room*)
Helen I didn't want to disturb you …
Nell No, that's all right. I was just having a coffee.
Helen Do you mind if I have one? I've been up most of the night.
Nell Certainly. Come and sit down.

Helen joins Nell on the swing seat

(*With a nervous laugh*) Look — two cups. John's been gone months and I'm still putting out two cups. Help yourself. I won't be a moment. I've got something on the stove. (*She moves towards the house*)

George enters on to the terrace from the house, also wearing a bathrobe

George (*beaming*) What a lovely morning. What a lovely morning for going into yonder thicket and having my way with thee. (*He throws off his robe; he has nothing on underneath but his underpants*)

During the following, Helen appears from behind the canopy

Ay, why not? Come, my lady, into yonder ferns where I may embrace your proud beauty and garland thee with flowers … (*His voice dies away as he sees Helen*)

George Helen!

Helen George. (*Pause*) Put your bathrobe on — you look faintly ridiculous.

George (*hurriedly replacing his bathrobe*) What is it?

Helen I'm sorry, George. Bad news. Your father's taken a turn for the worst. He had another fall. They took him into hospital early this morning.

George Oh. (*He glances at Nell*) I'll get dressed.

George exits

Nell You'd better have that coffee.

Nell and Helen sit. Nell pours the coffee

Helen I'd have rung but I think your phone's out of order …

Nell Oh. How did you know he was here? Did Jim tell you? Jim Grant?

Helen Jim Grant? No. Well, someone did ring last night to tell me where George was — which I thought was rather strange. But it wasn't necessary. I knew.

Nell What?

Helen I always know where George is. I have to — what with his father falling down all the … And then there's the children. We always tell each other where we're going.

Nell (*staring*) Then you knew about us.

Helen Oh, yes. Not straight away, but eventually. He told me. He usually tells me. George hates deceit.

Nell (*incredulously*) Does he? But you didn't say anything.

Helen What's the point? It's not as if it's the first time and one has to be civilized about these things.

Nell Civilized! I wouldn't be civilized.

Helen I know you wouldn't. But I try to keep up appearances.

Nell For Muffin, Puffin and Pumpkin?

Helen Yes.

Nell I still don't understand. Why was George so desperate you shouldn't find out if you knew already? Why did he convince me we were deceiving you?

Helen That's George's way. You see, then he doesn't have to come to a
decision. He can string you along. Besides, I think he rather enjoys it.

Nell (*quietly*) The rat — as my sister would say.

Helen It's not entirely his fault. (*She hesitates, then:*) Some years ago I was
a member of a badminton club. I met someone. And when I said I was
playing badminton — I was with someone else.

Nell (*with a rueful smile*) Not you as well, Helen. Tell me, does anyone
actually play sport in this country any more?

Helen George found out. He never quite forgave me. Now he feels he has
the right … I don't see the man any more but George still … (*She shrugs
her shoulders*)

Nell Messes around?

Helen Yes. (*She takes out her handkerchief*) Funny — I thought I'd got used
to it. Now I'm going to cry. (*She rises abruptly and crosses the terrace*) I
still love him, you see. Bloody silly, isn't it? Tell him I'll be at the hospital.

Helen exits L through the garden

*Nell stares after Helen for a moment and then goes into the drawing-room
and reconnects the phone*

*Jim enters the terrace from L. He follows Nell into the drawing-room,
looking pleased*

Nell turns from the phone

Jim I was in the garden. I saw her leave.

Nell Yes.

Jim She seemed distressed.

Nell She was. You told her, didn't you?

Jim (*after a hesitation*) What makes you think that?

Nell Someone rang her last night. It was you, wasn't it, Jim?

Jim (*after a pause*) I didn't have to tell her. She knew. So who was making
empty gestures last night. That's what I came over to tell you.

Nell Some people might say that was a little ruthless, Jim …

Jim (*straightening a picture*) I simply wanted to enlighten you about
George.

Nell (*regarding Jim thoughtfully*) You've certainly enlightened me. First,
the inscription in the book of poems, then Mrs Williams, and finally Helen.
I've very few illusions left about George Rush.

Jim Good. Then it's time you discouraged him.

Nell I've done my best, Jim. But he keeps coming back. I don't think I shall
ever be free of him. You've tried everything and he's still here. What else
can we do?

Jim (*after a pause*) There is something else …

Nell Is there? What?

Jim You don't have to know …

Nell No, tell me.

Jim I know a couple of governors at his school. I know he's up for promotion. I thought a word in the right quarter — a little pressure from above …

Nell Brilliant. He's always been concerned about his career.

Jim (*smiling*) That's what I thought. Look, I suppose you want to get rid of him. Should I come back later?

Nell No, don't come back later, Jim.

Jim (*staring*) What?

Nell I can forgive most things — possibly even the ruthlessness. What I couldn't forgive was that self-satisfied smirk just now. You're a cold fish, Jim. You lack feeling.

Jim How can you say that? Remember the first time we met? I wept.

Nell I can do that to people.

Jim You know why I wept. It was for her.

Nell Are you sure it wasn't for yourself? Tyrants can weep, Jim.

Jim You think I'm a tyrant?

Nell I think you could be. And I don't want to be around to find out.

Jim That's a terrible thing to say.

Nell I know. I am terrible. That's why my husband left me. Didn't they tell you? When I'm angry I'm a sight to behold, Jim.

Jim I don't know why you're angry. You've no future with him. And you're not getting any younger.

Nell Thanks for pointing that out, Jim.

Jim You'll be alone, Nell. Have you thought of that?

Nell There are worse things than being on your own, Jim. There's being alone while you're living with someone else. And don't mention the money.

Jim I suppose you find that humiliating.

Nell No, I find it too tempting.

Jim I don't understand. Is this because I was prepared to fight for you?

Nell No, I didn't mind the fighting. What I couldn't stand was the thought of you straightening these bloody pictures for the rest of my life! (*She circles the room pushing the pictures awry*)

Jim (*staring in astonishment*) I think I'd better go. I'll come back when you're in a more reasonable state of mind … (*He goes on to the terrace*)

Nell (*following Jim*) You'll have a long wait. I haven't been in a reasonable state of mind for years…

Jim moves to the terrace exit L

Oh, and Jim.

Jim turns

If you do call again — come to the front door. Don't assume you have the right to walk through my garden.

Jim exits angrily

  Gail enters R. *She is carrying a handbag*

Nell turns round and almost bumps into Gail

Gail (*after a pause*) That's not working out, is it?
Nell What are you doing here?
Gail I've been trying to reach you all morning.
Nell What is it?
Gail It's Terry. He wanted to get in touch with you.
Nell On a Saturday? Oh dear. What about?
Gail He didn't say. But he didn't look very pleased. You haven't broken anything else have you?
Nell No. (*Pause*) I've lost a file.
Gail I thought he seemed morose.
Nell He's always morose.
Gail He's more morose than usual. His divorce came through this week.
Nell He should be dancing in the streets.
Gail Why are all you married people so cynical? I asked Terry what it felt like to be divorced. Do you know what he said? "Ever walked a mile with a stone in your shoe and then taken it out? That's what it's like." I mean, what have you all got against marriage?
Nell I notice you're not rushing into it.
Gail I haven't met the right man — I've always been too busy.
Nell That's not the reason, is it? It's me, isn't it? I'm a dreadful warning — like something swinging from a gibbet and rattling its chains.
Gail No — I'd get married tomorrow if I met the right man.
Nell That's easy to say.
Gail (*mysteriously*) In fact, I may have met him.
Nell (*intrigued*) Who is he?
Gail I'm not telling you. All I'm saying is I don't think you should let one bad experience put you off marriage.
Nell How many do you need?
Gail You're brooding again. Why don't you come out with us tonight. Paula from Claims has got tickets to a séance.
Nell A what?
Gail Sort of a spiritualist meeting — should be fun. There's a medium. You can ask her questions.

Nell I wonder if she knows where that file is.
Gail No … Questions about dead people — if they're happy, that sort of thing.
Nell I don't want to ask questions about dead people.
Gail Paula says you meet some very interesting types.
Nell Not much point in them being interesting if they're dead.
Gail I mean the widowers.
Nell Gail, I've already met one widower and it wasn't much fun.
Gail Well, it would certainly be better than sitting around here on your own …

George enters from the drawing-room. He looks uncomfortably at Gail

Gail gives George a cold stare

George Hallo, Gail.
Gail George.
George Seen my jacket, Nell?
Nell In the hall cupboard.

George exits

Gail What's he doing here?
Nell Mending a fuse.
Gail You're such a fool, Nell.
Nell I know.

There is the sound of a mobile phone ringing

Nell rises

Gail It's all right — it's mine. (*She takes a mobile phone from her bag. Into the phone*) Hallo? … Oh. Hallo, Terry. … Yes, well actually, I'm sitting with her at the moment …

Nell shakes her head

Yes. I'll get her.

Gail hands the phone to Nell

He wants to speak to you.
Nell (*into the phone*) Hallo, Terry. If it's about the file … . No, I didn't. … What? … Oh. … Well, I don't know. … No, I haven't. … Yes, I am

surprised. Look, can I ring you back in a few minutes? I've got some home-made jam boiling over...

Nell returns the phone to Gail, who puts it down

Gail (*sighing*) Home-made jam. Why do you have to be so flippant? He doesn't like it.
Nell He must do. He's just asked me to go to the races with him.
Gail What! But you're not his type.
Nell No.
Gail It's not fair. You have one man in the garden, one in the bedroom, and another one asking you to the races. And I was feeling sorry for you.
Nell Oh dear — it's him, isn't it?
Gail What?
Nell The man in your life.
Gail Certainly not. He doesn't shave and he sleeps in his suits. I'm going. (*She moves across the terrace towards the exit and turns*) You'll need a swing door on that bedroom.
Nell I didn't say I was going.
Gail I'm not worried.
Nell Aren't you. (*She smiles*) You've forgotten your phone, Gail.

Gail returns and picks up her phone

Nell Don't use it on the motorway, Gail. Keep both hands on the wheel. After all, you're my only sister and I don't want you meeting the dear departed before the séance.

George enters the drawing-room

Gail turns to look in George's direction. She gives him a long, hard glare. She unexpectedly kisses Nell on the cheek

Gail (*lowering her voice*) I want you to go, Nell. I don't mind.
Nell Are you sure.
Gail Yes. After all, you are more his age ...

Nell smiles

Besides, it's the only way you're going to keep that job...

Gail exits around the side of the house

Nell goes into the drawing-room

George I rang the hospital from the bedroom. Apparently he's stable.

Nell So you rang from the bedroom. Was that after you reconnected the phone?

George I didn't want us to be disturbed.

Nell We were disturbed.

George I'm sorry.

Nell Helen's been trying to ring all night. (*Innocently*) What I can't understand is how she knew you were here.

George (*cautiously*) Didn't she say?

Nell No.

George Do you know what I think? I think he told her.

Nell Do you mean Jim?

George Yes. It's the sort of thing he'd do.

Nell That's what I thought.

George Yes, it was Jim all right. Did I see him leaving the garden just now?

Nell Yes.

George I thought so. No matter how bright the day some bugger always turns up to spoil it.

Nell I sent him away.

George For good?

Nell Yes.

George (*grinning*) Poor old Jim. Another entry in that dusty ledger. Account closed due to poor returns. Loss to be written off against tax.

Nell Isn't that a bit cruel?

George He deserves it. He's a bastard.

Nell If we're voting on bastards, George — you get mine. (*She dumps the carrier bag of George's possessions in his arms*)

George What?

Nell She knew, George. She's always known. It's a game you two play. So when you dared Jim to ring her last night — you were just grandstanding. It's an open marriage, isn't it?

George (*after a hesitation*) Well, not exactly open.

Nell But not closed.

George No.

Nell Sort of ajar?

George I suppose you think I'm a hypocrite?

Nell Got it in one.

George All right — what's wrong with a little hypocrisy?

Nell (*aghast*) Don't you know?

George All I know is that it's the hypocrites that keep the world turning. We're the ones who have to fetch the bunnies' ears and walk the dog. It's the hypocrite who mows the lawn, fixes the roof and pays the rent.

Nell And it's the hypocrite who has the best of both worlds, George.

George (*bitterly*) You call this the best? No, that's for the divorcees with their Mark Two wives. Darling this and darling that and "Have you met my lovely wife? We're so much in love". Of course they are — they've only just bloody started.

Nell Why didn't you tell me she knew?

George (*sighing*) Because I knew you'd want more …

Nell More? More of what?

George More of everything.

Nell You mean more love?

George The trouble is you want me body and soul, Nell.

Nell It's the only way I know, George.

George I do love you.

Nell Then go home and write a poem about it.

George Look, we've been through this before: the tears, the recriminations, the reconciliations — and we always end up ——

Nell Crashing into the quilt?

George — making love.

Nell Yes, but the trouble is you only want it on a part-time basis. You're like an auxiliary fireman, George — you only turn out for the big blaze. Now take your things and go.

George I don't have to go straight away. (*He glances slyly at his watch*) They said he was stable.

Nell Then he's the only one around here who is.

George Things are going to be different, Nell. (*He puts down the carrier bag*)

Nell You've said that before.

George I think we can manage a trip later in the year. Possibly a weekend.

Nell Two whole days! Well, that should keep me going until you pop down the chimney at Christmas.

George grows in confidence and puts his arms around her

George I love you, Nell.

Nell I love you, George.

George kisses Nell and holds her tight. She surreptitiously looks at her watch. Slowly he becomes aware of this

George (*shocked*) You're looking at your watch.

Nell Was I?

George Yes.

Nell Well, I have to ring someone.

George Who?

Nell Terry. He wants to take me to the races this afternoon.
George Oh. You should go. Do you good.
Nell You don't mind?
George No.
Nell No — you'd even do us a packed lunch, wouldn't you?
George What?

The phone rings. Nell answers it

George listens to the call

Nell (*into the phone*) Hallo? Terry? … Yes. Yes, I'd love to go. Nice of you
to ask me. … Afterwards? Why not? (*She notices that George is listening*)
One moment, Terry. I've just got to put the cat out …

*Nell puts the phone down, picks up the carrier bag and shoves it into George's
arms*

Nell propels George out of the hall door, then returns to the phone

(*Into the phone*) Hallo, Terry — that cat's got to go. … About two? That
would be fine. Oh, and Terry, don't wear that suit. … You don't mind me
saying that? …That's what you like about me? You like plain speaking?
(*She grins broadly*) Then you're going to like me, Terry … (*She continues
talking, her voice fading and becoming inaudible*)

The Lights fade

CURTAIN

FURNITURE AND PROPERTY LIST

ACT I

SCENE 1

On stage: LIVING ROOM
On shelves: books including cookbook
Sofa
Easy chairs
Coffee table. *On it*: letter
Sideboard. *On it*: tray of drinks, glasses, phone, answering machine.
     Two drinks ready-poured for **Nell**

TERRACE
Swing seat with canopy
Iron coffee table
Table
Chairs
Iron golf club

Personal: **George**: watch (worn throughout)

SCENE 2

On stage: TERRACE
On table: jug of lemonade, glasses

Off stage: Battered briefcase containing slim volume of poetry (**George**)
Brochure (**Jim**)

Personal: **Jim**: handkerchief

SCENE 3

Re-set: **George**'s volume of poetry on sideboard

Off stage: Handbag containing bottle of tablets; coat (**Nell**)

ACT II

SCENE 1

On stage: TERRACE
             On swing seat: **Jim**'s shirt
             Hoe
             Box of chocolates

Off stage: Tray with jug of lemonade and glasses (**Nell**)

Personal: **Jim**: piece of notepaper

SCENE 2

On stage: **Nell**'s handbag

Off stage: Carrier bag containing **George**'s belongings

Personal: **Nell**: earrings
             George: key

SCENE 3

Off stage: Tray with coffee pot and two cups on it (**Nell**)
             Handbag containing mobile phone (**Gail**)

Personal: **Nell**: sunglasses
             Helen: handkerchief

LIGHTING PLOT

Practical fittings required: nil
A drawing-room and terrace garden. The same throughout

ACT I, SCENE 1

To open: Drawing-room lights on; light fades from terrace thoughout scene

No cues

ACT I, SCENE 2

To open: Sunny afternoon lighting

No cues

ACT I, SCENE 3

To open: Darkness

Cue 1	When ready *Snap on drawing-room lights*	(Page 23)
Cue 2	**George** switches off the lights *Black-out*	(Page 30)
Cue 3	**Nell** switches the lights back on *Snap on drawing-room lights*	(Page 30)
Cue 4	**George** dims the drawing-room lights *Dim drawing-room lights*	(Page 30)
Cue 5	**George** heads for the garden exit *Security lights come on in garden*	(Page 30)

ACT II, SCENE 1

To open: Sunny afternoon lighting

No cues

ACT II, SCENE 2

To open: Drawing-room lights on; terrace in darkness

No cues

ACT II, SCENE 3

To open: Sunny morning lighting

Cue 6   **Nell**: " … going to like me, Terry …" (She continues   (Page 65)
              talking, her voice fading)
              Fade lights slowly

EFFECTS PLOT

ACT I

ACT II